MW00641409

PRAISE FOR
THE LOVE HABIT

"*The Love Habit* teaches a delicate balance of understanding who you are and navigating your way out of cultural loneliness. It addresses the importance of self-identity and its impact on forming healthy, meaningful relationships. *The Love Habit* embodies practical steps to shift cognitive thinking toward a holistic approach to healing. It captures how you can be in control of your own healing. I highly recommend *The Love Habit* to anyone looking to deepen their understanding of all that balance truly encompasses. This book will have a significant impact on its readers."

—**JuTone M. Lajoie**, LICSW, cofounder of
Time to Heal Counseling & Consulting

"This is the relationship book I've been needing! I wish I had read this thirty years ago but am so glad I have it now. In *The Love Habit*, Howard teaches us how to radically transform our lives by examining the attitudes and behaviors that are holding us back from stronger, healthier relationships, both personally and professionally. Howard's powerful messages inspire, uplift, and encourage readers, all while offering practical tips for creating the life you want and deserve. This is a book readers will return to again and again in their journeys to love themselves and others more fully."

—**Jennifer McGaha**, author of *The Joy Document: Creating a Midlife of Surprise and Delight, Bushwhacking: How to Get Lost in the Woods and Write Your Way Out,* and *Flat Broke with Two Goats*

"A practical and actionable guide to transforming outdated patterns and habits to create a brighter and happier future full of meaningful relationships and love."

—**Amy B. Scher**, bestselling author of *How to Heal Yourself When No One Else Can*

"In a time when the systems of power are swirling with destruction trying to tear at the fabric of our communities and the seams of our very souls, it becomes a matter of survival that we find ways to love on one another and ourselves. Love becomes a revolutionary force. *The Love Habit* is needed now more than ever."

—**Lydia Wylie-Kellermann**, author of *This Sweet Earth: Walking with Our Children in the Age of Climate Collapse* and editor of *The Sandbox Revolution: Raising Kids for a Just World*

THE LOVE HABIT

THE LOVE HABIT

RAINIE HOWARD

DAILY SELF-CARE PRACTICES FOR A
HAPPIER LIFE & HEALTHIER RELATIONSHIPS

Broadleaf Books
Minneapolis

THE LOVE HABIT
Daily Self-Care Practices for a Happier Life & Healthier Relationships

30 29 28 27 26 25 24   1 2 3 4 5 6 7 8 9

Library of Congress Cataloging-in-Publication Data

Names: Howard, Rainie, author.
Title: The love habit : daily self-care practices for a happier life
    and healthier relationships / by Rainie Howard.
Description: Minneapolis : Broadleaf Books, [2023] | Includes
    bibliographical references.
Identifiers: LCCN 2023058913 (print) | LCCN 2023058914 (ebook) |
    ISBN 9781506496740 (hardback) | ISBN 9781506498041 (ebook)
Subjects: LCSH: Self-perception. | Self-esteem. | Interpersonal relations.
Classification: LCC BF697.5.S43 H6936 2023 (print) | LCC BF697.5.S43
    (ebook) | DDC 158.2—dc23/eng/20240102
LC record available at https://lccn.loc.gov/2023058913
LC ebook record available at https://lccn.loc.gov/2023058914

Cover design: 1517 Media

Print ISBN: 978-1-5064-9674-0
eBook ISBN: 978-1-5064-9804-1

CONTENTS

PART III: UNLOCKING YOUR DISCERNMENT—ALIGN, EXECUTE, AND IMPACT

Higher Self Relationship Model

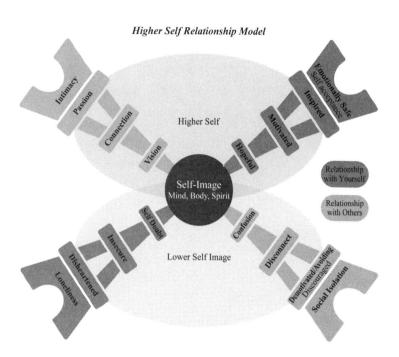

PREFACE

There is a way to live a better life. The better way is hidden in your daily routine. It's in the management of your emotions, expectations, and relationships. It's becoming the love you desire and having conversations with the energy of peace you want to experience.

I'm Rainie Howard, and for over a decade I've been passionate about studying human behavior. My journey started with the desire to understand and empower myself through life's struggles. After applying what I learned, I wanted to share my wisdom with others. This led to an amazing career as a relationship coach and bestselling author, sharing the wisdom and knowledge I've gained to help people all over the world live fully.

***

Perhaps there is some part of your life where you feel the need to resolve issues that have spilled over from the past or a season of rebuilding. Perhaps there are people you need to distance yourself from or even people you need to bring closer to fortify your deepest relationships. Through lessons on love, mental wellness, and caring for the entirety of our spirit and body we can take control of our realities.

If our self-image defines our relationship experiences with others, how do we improve it? If we are subconsciously teaching people how to treat us, what can we do to gain more respect? How are our daily habits creating our destiny? What is "toxic"? What are "alpha males"? What is love? Does it exist? What are the terms being used online, which have now spilled over into our everyday lives, that warp our sense of ourselves and others in relationships? Who are the top influencers speaking about issues in romantic relationships? What should we take away from this online content and new social norms? Should we take anything?

To be in healthy relationships, whether with a friend, at work, or in a romantic partnership, we must first start with the relationship we have with ourselves. Without addressing this missing piece of how we relate to ourselves, we end up perpetually stuck in unhealthy friendships, romantic relationships, and more but also engaged in a pattern of repeatedly inviting new unhealthy relationships into our lives. Enjoying a quality relationship starts with habitually maintaining a healthy lifestyle, which includes creating a routine for your spiritual, mental, and physical health. This is all essential for a positive self-image that lends itself toward a healthier self, spirit, and community.

I want you—yes, *you*—to get the most out of *The Love Habit*. Since the publication of my book *Addicted To Pain* in 2016, I've coached thousands of women looking to improve their relationships; careers, parenting, and partnering are priorities for so many people, but for women we often seek to nurture, putting everyone and everything ahead of our own needs. This leads to exhaustion and self-depletion. In 2018 I was past my wits' end. My kids came home to a mother who was depressed, stressed, and unhappy. I hid it from them; I would pick them up from school and pretend I was ok by asking, "How was your day?" After they would respond I would go back into my invisible shell of silence. My husband could tell I wasn't at my best when I was no longer interested in watching our favorite Saturday night comedy show; instead I would lay in bed for hours and cry uncontrollably. He tried to build me up, and he would hold me while I cried, but we both knew I had to work on myself. So, I paid special attention to what I consumed regarding media, food, and conversation. I had to also gain more control of my emotions. And so, I changed. Through measured techniques, you will change and learn discernment so that you don't ever experience the absolute bottom I've felt myself.

***

I'm able to look back from this point in my life and say that I've been blessed, truly and lovingly—a fact that I don't take lightly and that enabled me to write this book for those of us—many of us—who are interested in moving beyond identifying our problem areas to form better habits so that we're able to develop the healthiest possible versions of ourselves. Don't wait until you finish *The Love Habit* to act. You've picked up this book intending to change; today, promise yourself you will plant the seeds you need to blossom.

INTRODUCTION

Did you know that you can become addicted to living a life you don't like? This is what happens when you continue thinking the same way, having the same conversations, making the same choices, and doing the same thing. You reproduce the same experiences that get you the same life results. You are conditioned to do something so many times that your body knows how to do it better than your conscious mind.

I know this well because I lived it. This was my life. The first thirty-five years of my life consisted of automatic habits programmed from childhood, resulting in an unfulfilled life. It wasn't until I reached a breaking point in my life that things begin to change for me. My change occurred during a time when everything seemed broken. My health was in jeopardy—I had severe anxiety, depression, and rapid weight gain. I had insomnia and panic attacks, I struggled financially, and I was mentally and emotionally unstable. I found myself crying uncontrollably for no apparent reason, my relationships were broken, I struggled as a wife and mother, I struggled with low self-esteem, and I didn't like who I had become. I wasn't happy with my life, and I wanted transformation and change badly, but I felt stuck even after working hard. I had put my all into being better, having more, and accomplishing greater things. I had successfully grown several businesses, completed my master's degree, bought and sold our first home, and had been married for over ten years. My life was consumed and busy with many tasks that I continued to complete daily despite the overwhelming sense of despair I felt.

On the outside, everything looked great. People admired me and would often compliment me on my success. No one knew how badly I was struggling on the inside, and I had no idea I was about to enter the battle of my life. During this season in my life, I noticed a big change. Something was different; life felt different; there was a shift in my environment. It felt like I was at a crossroads in my life. I was at the intersection of my life facing two roads—one road would be the path of no change or transformation, just a dead-end street, and the other path was the path of the unknown leading to a new, revived, adventurous life. I understood that the choices I made would determine the destiny of my life. I had lived in the same home for almost ten years, but I knew it was time to move. My business had been progressing in a strategy that was working successfully, but I knew it was time to transition and innovate a new plan. My marriage had achieved over a decade of love, but I knew there was unresolved tension within the relationship I shared with my husband.

I felt a strong urgency for transformation, and I knew that I had to be committed to changing myself first to change my life.

There are times in your life when your habits create results you may not like but you're able to live with, and then there are times when repeated habits become unbearable and lead to severe, life-altering results that shape your entire existence. I understood that I was in a season in my life that required mandatory transformation.

When your body, mind, and emotions automatically know how to keep doing what you've always done, getting what you've always got, the biggest habit you need to break is the habit of being the person you've allowed yourself to become. I was fully aware that I needed to think differently, speak differently, and take different actions in order to create a different life. Your thoughts give life to your imagination, and your imagination gives life to your words, and your words direct your behavior. Every thought creates a chemical reaction that becomes a belief and leads to making choices and decisions that shape your entire life. In my discovery process I learned that my subconscious feelings of inadequacy led to a lack of self-love which automatically created situations and relationships that led to a life that I did not like. And to free myself of the emotional baggage and pain, I began to connect to the ultimate universal energy of love, through gratitude and a daily commitment to nurturing my mental, physical, and emotional health. This process is what I call *the love habit*. It's a habitual commitment to choosing to prioritize yourself holistically in mind, body, and spirit by aligning yourself with appreciation, peace, and joy above all else. This self-care practice connects you to a happier life engaging in healthier relationships.

A habit is the consistent accumulation of action that is birthed after you've done something so many times that your body knows how to do it better than your conscious mind because it has been programmed subconsciously. Creating new daily habits can feel challenging in the beginning, but through consistency they become a natural, effortless way of life. The *love habit* is less about adding to your life and more about releasing and unlearning habits and behaviors that no longer serve you.

During our childhood, we are subconsciously programmed to fear, doubt, struggle, and suffer. According to data from Harvard University, the brain develops rapidly during the first years of life. Our subconscious mind is being programmed during the first seven years of our lives, and our brain is working in the theta state. The theta state is when the brain subconsciously downloads programming based on the environment around us. If a child's environment consisted of people who were stressed, fearful, discontent with life, or feeling victimized, as children we also learned how to experience life with a victim's conscience.

A victim mindset will force a person to habitually seek out external situations and people to blame for feelings of love and pain. This is the result of a belief that both your happiness and unfulfillment are due to the outside world circumstances.

> Your perception of any given thing, at any given moment, can influence the brain chemistry, which, in turn, affects the environment where your cells reside and controls their

fate. Perception is awareness shaped by belief. Beliefs "control" perception. Rewrite perception and you rewrite genes and behavior. I am free to change how I respond to the world, so as I change the way I see the world I change my genetic expression. We are not victims of our genes. We are masters of our genetics.—Dr. Bruce Lipton, Ph.D., cellular biologist

The belief that life is happening to us and is out of our control paralyzes the adult who learned to view the world through the lens of chronic victimhood. Though a person doesn't choose victimhood, they are solely responsible for observing the problems that exist in their life and building a practice beyond the unhealthy reality of their present.

In this book you will learn how to evolve from a victim mindset into an empowered growth mindset as a victorious creator in your life. At the end of each chapter, you will have an opportunity to reflect on *the love habit* technique (LOVE is an acronym for Listen, Optimize, Validate, and Experience) and how it applies to the key message, leading to a list of questions you can journal and ask yourself.

This book is divided into three parts:

I. Reinventing Yourself—Create the Life You Want

II. Habit Techniques—Think, Believe, Expect, and Become

III. Unlocking Discernment—Align, Execute, and Impact

REINVENTING YOURSELF

In the first part of the book, you will learn how to reinvent yourself by first understanding yourself and your personality and creating the life you want and desire. We often believe that since we are good and nice, we should be immune to painful experiences and relationships. Being nice to others should automatically result in others being nice to us. When we give our loyalty and faithfulness to another person, in return we expect them to be loyal and faithful to us. But this is not the case in every situation or relationship, and when asked, "What lessons were learned from a negative relationship experience and what can be done differently?" victims of these negative relationships often say, "I was too nice. I'm just too nice with people." What that means is, "I allowed mistreatment while being nice and showing that I cared even though I was hurt." In the first part of the book, you will discover the hidden ways you are subconsciously teaching people how to treat you. It all comes down to your specific personality. Trying hard to please people is an unhealthy habit. You can never control what another person thinks about you. Therefore, working hard to please people and to gain their approval is self-betrayal. It's time to free yourself of the bondage of external validation.

Freedom is the only worthy goal in life. It is won by disregarding things that lie beyond our control. Stop aspiring to be anyone other than your own best self: for that does fall within your control.— Epictetus

The one thing we don't have control of is what others think about us. Freedom is inextricably linked to our perceptions of how other people see and react to us. It's time to courageously release old patterns that have been holding you back from the life and relationships you desire. The *love habit* is a vehicle designed to help you better understand how to use life's experiences to create a new and improved life while discovering the authentic self in a one-on-one healthy relationship with the person in the mirror.

HABIT TECHNIQUES

The second part of this book will help you discover and change the stories you've created about yourself that have shaped your self-image and identity. You will discover the science behind developing techniques to form healthy self-image; how your thoughts, feelings, and expectations impact your life and relationships; and why using habitual techniques for quality connection and alignment is essential. Your daily repetition, routine, and habits dictate who you are and who you will become. Every time you feed a habit, it gets stronger, and what you starve will weaken. You can weaken a habit by not repeating it. We all have a personal narrative or life story that we replay in our mind. Sometimes that story may reinforce limiting beliefs about your growth or improvement. However, you can change that demotivating story and nurture and empower your ideal self through self-image techniques. Imagine developing the skills to identify and overcome negative emotional habits, such as the fear of abandonment due to past relationships issues like heartbreak, separation, or divorce. You can now gain the knowledge and strategy to master your emotions: acknowledge and identify the beliefs, learn the lesson behind your life results, and imagine yourself overcoming all mental limitations. Your new habits will empower you both personally and professionally. In Chapter 6, I share strategies on how to prioritize yourself at work and gain the most value as the leader of your life and career, building self-trust and overcoming people pleasing tendencies.

Habit techniques—Think, Believe, Expect, and Become.

DISCERNMENT

In the third part of the book, you will learn how to identify deception and manipulation by developing techniques for discernment and good character judgment. It's time to learn the secret technique of creating daily habits to enhance mental and emotional happiness—the key to having a great relationship with yourself and with others. We all have the human desires for certainty, adventure, feelings of importance, and love. Having your desires and needs met is very important. The balance of certainty, adventure, feelings of importance, and love are the secret components that create happiness. As you implement the daily intuitive techniques shared in this book, you will develop a more positive mindset that will result in quality, connected, and positive relationships. It's important to understand that not every feeling and every thought has to dictate your state of being. You have the power to gain control of your thoughts, emotions, and feelings. No matter what you're going through in your life, you can elevate yourself above the battlefield. In order to do this, you must first declutter and detoxify your mind of negativity. This clearing process can vary for different people, but it's best to do what works best for you. This is a process of healing and releasing resentment and other negative emotions that weigh you down. Understanding your intuition, your subtle desires, and your inspirations, and knowing how to be guided and directed internally, will support you in gaining clarity in making decisions.

As you stay grounded in your core values and beliefs, this will also support you in setting boundaries, saying no when it's necessary, meaning what you say, and practicing self-control. You must believe in your truth and the importance of following the path of your life. This requires a level of connection with your intuitive thoughts and a soft inner voice. It's becoming a fan of yourself and life-long supporter of your mind, body, and spirit. Your intuition is the guiding wisdom that shows you the way to go when you're uncertain about what decision to make. It's when those small moments of life need your attention. Your mind, body, and emotions are connected; therefore it's important to honor every aspect of yourself and make time to connect with yourself fully.

PART I

REINVENTING YOURSELF—
CREATE THE LIFE YOU WANT

1 | NICE PEOPLE GET HURT TOO

We've all felt it before; we just didn't know how to verbalize it enough to get real clear answers. You know that feeling; it's a lonely feeling, the feeling of not being understood. It's the feeling that life is withholding vital information about your truth, and you have no clue on how to unlock the keys to your soul. It's when our beliefs don't match the results of our reality. You believe that since you are nice, people should be nice to you, and you should be immune to painful relationships. When you give your loyalty and faithfulness to another person, in return you expect them to be loyal and faithful to you. But this is not the case in every relationship, and life doesn't always seem fair. Trying to be nice all the time, being a people pleaser, and putting everyone and everything above yourself doesn't result in your personal fulfillment. These behaviors come from the purpose of gaining other people's approval. However, when it comes to living a life you desire and of your purpose, it may require you to say *no* when it's necessary and to make the choice to acknowledge your needs and health over servicing another person, and also putting yourself first.

However, many of us struggle to prioritize ourselves because when we do, it's followed by feelings of guilt and shame.

But have you ever stopped and asked yourself, "What if being too nice causes you to lose yourself?" Beginning in childhood, we are systematically programmed to be nice, share our toys, and smile when someone compliments us. Society's standards teach that being nice is the way to go if you want people to like you. However, trying to be nice may often mean lying to others about what you think and how you feel, and being too nice can cause extreme people pleasing. While there's nothing wrong with being nice, the issue occurs when we intentionally commit ourselves to the "I'm nice personality," solely to gain the approval and validation of others. This is when "being nice" becomes less about building healthy relationships and more about getting people to see you in a certain way. This can lead to you shifting your identity to appease others resulting in you losing your true authentic self. In our world of social media, we are rewarded for how many likes and followers we have. When you post something that other people enjoy, you gain public approval, and when you post opinions or content that people may agree with, you can gain lots of followers. People are rewarded on social media the more others approve of them, which can motivate unhealthy people-pleasing behaviors. This has resulted in many people losing sight of authentic self-awareness, and instead of fulfilling personal goals, we become distracted by the influence of others. Could this lead to a "need to please," and instead of addressing necessary conflict, we prefer to be nice?

It needs to be understood that being nice doesn't always means being kind. Kindness is the quality expressed in being friendly to others due to the habitual consistency of being a friend to yourself. But even after being kind to others, you may find yourself wondering why kindness isn't always reciprocated. It's the same as when bad things happen to good people; we all want to know *why*. How can a mother verbally abuse and demean one daughter but excessively compliment and praise her other daughter? How can a boss respect and admire one worker yet despise another? How can a man lie, cheat, and betray one woman and later settle down to marry and be faithful to another? Why are people different with different people? Have you ever found yourself wondering why you had to go through that terrible relationship, why you dealt with so much trauma in your childhood, why you're still single after so many years, or why you struggle with loneliness and pain? You may also wonder why one of your relationships or friendships ended and why you experienced so much betrayal. You may be asking yourself, *why me, why now*?

As nice as you are, as hard as you work, and as much as you give, you might still find yourself in unwanted, low-quality relationships with people who don't value you. You notice how they treat you differently. You might even second guess your own perceptions or feelings.

No, that's my friend, and she really cares for me. That's my mom; she's only hard on me because she wants what's best for me. My manager only treats me that way because I need to work harder. I'm not doing enough. I need to give more, I need to work longer, and I need to be better.

Imagine how this self-blame and judgment can impact you mentally, emotionally, and physically. Justifying a broken heart and mistreatment with thoughts of inadequacy becomes a way of life. But whose fault is it? Who can you blame for the feeling of defeat? *It's my fault* (you blame yourself and feel unloved), *it's his fault* (you blame your ex), *it's their fault* (you blame your parents), and when those don't work . . . maybe you blame situations, others, your relationships, or even God and the Universe.

How can you have such great desire and passion for an amazing life full of love, happiness, and abundance, but experience a reality defined by the misery of unhealthy relationships? You are good to people, so why aren't they good to you? You may find yourself saying, "Why am I so unhappy when I work so hard to make others happy? When will I experience the joy of life?" Instead, you are faced with more disappointment. You feel the conflict of your dreams saying yes but the reality of your life screaming no. That was my own experience. I believed that being nice, reliable, and supportive toward others would improve my relationships and influence others to treat me better. However, my personality habits were teaching others to mistreat, use, and take advantage of me. This is what led me to learn about the personality habits that attract negative relationships. I'm going to share these self-sabotaging personality habits with you now.

PERSONALITY HABITS THAT ENABLE PAIN AND SUFFERING

There are many ways in which we subconsciously contribute to attracting painful relationships. But people who are empathic— considered "sensitive," or very tuned into the feelings of others— may be most at risk. As an empath, you don't just feel *for* people, you feel *with* people by taking in others' emotions. You go out of your way to help others, and it may feel extremely bad or disappointing when you're not able to. Helping others and giving of yourself may sometimes seem like a positive trait, but these habits often lead to toxic relationships.

The following list includes personality habits that you might recognize in yourself. When embodied excessively, these seven characteristic behaviors invite negative relationships. I'm going to help you identify the habits you are falling prey to, and then I'll offer solutions on how to exchange them for more positive habits.

1. The "I'm always here to listen, so call me anytime" personality

2. The "I'm going to say yes even though I want to say no" personality

3. The "I'm an excellent problem solver and perfectionist" personality

4. The "I'm your number-one helper so you can rely on me always" personality

5. The "I'm an overachiever so I can make anything work" personality

6. The "I'm loyal and committed no matter what" personality

7. The "I'm a peacemaker" personality

Before we go into these habits, I want you to know there is no quick fix. Real change happens with real dedication and full commitment to a daily practice. Let's go into each of these habits so you can truly understand what they are and how they might be affecting you negatively. Then I'm going to show you how to shift these patterns for a happier you and more successful relationships with those around you.

THE *I'M ALWAYS HERE TO LISTEN, SO CALL ME ANYTIME* PERSONALITY

Do you always find yourself leaning in with a listening ear, going out of your way to serve and support other people even though you have big struggles and challenges in your personal life? People who love to gossip and talk about their problems love the *"I'm always here to listen so call me anytime" personality*. However, this type of engagement can be exhausting and toxic. This personality habit not only invites gossipers and people who often talk bad about others, it also subconsciously creates the possibility of becoming the victim of gossip. It creates the underlying thought that, "If this person is so comfortable talking to me about another person, they can be just as comfortable gossiping about me to someone else." If you find yourself struggling with this habit, I want to encourage you to implement *the triple-A technique plan*. This technique will help you identify the root cause behind the negative habit.

The triple-A technique plan

- ◆ **A**cknowledge: Understand your personality habits and how they impact your relationships.

- ◆ **A**sk why? Journal the question, "Why do I believe I struggle with that negative habit?" Learn from your past and admit your responsibility to take ownership of your healing and personal growth.

- ◆ **A**pply your vision: How would you like to be in relationships? Visualize yourself in the ideal role and begin to practice the habits that support your ideal personality habit.

As you first acknowledge your struggle with people pleasing and always feeling the need to give a listening ear to gossip and negative conversations, this leads to the awareness of the habit. Then you can start asking yourself why you have a habit of people pleasing. After journaling reasons why you may struggle with that habit, you may discover that your real issue is not your relationship with people. It could be the feelings of guilt—thinking that you're not being a good friend if you end the toxic conversation, so out of guilt you allow the unwanted gossip. You could also feel bored with your life, and gossiping and listening to another person's problems is toxic yet entertaining. Wanting to overly give of yourself and appease another person is another driving force behind the personality. Unhealed traumas, insecurity, and feelings of not being enough all connect to habitually overextending yourself. Finally, you can create a new vision that serves you and your relationships better. By asking the question, "How would you like to be in relationships?" you now understand you desire having healthier boundaries that eliminate gossiping by excusing yourself from a conversation that feels toxic. Now visualize yourself in the role of setting healthy relationship boundaries.

THE *I'M GOING TO SAY YES EVEN THOUGH I WANT TO SAY NO* PERSONALITY

People with a low self-image often find themselves struggling to say no, due to the fear of others thinking they're not generous enough. If you struggle with the guilt and shame of saying no, you are subconsciously and consciously teaching people that you are a people pleaser by always saying yes. You don't want to hurt their feelings or let them down, but you are unaware that you're creating a reputation of always saying yes, which can lead others to believe you are a pushover and they can get whatever they need from you. There are people who only want a relationship with you because of what you can do for them, and when you are no longer providing the value they want from you, the relationship is over. Unfortunately, this personality trait attracts a lifetime of users and opportunists. Awareness of habits within relationships can prevent the hurt and pain of these types of relationships.

Here's an example of implementing *the triple-A technique plan* to overcome the *I'm going to say yes even though I want to say no* personality:

- **A**cknowledge—create an awareness of your habits of always saying yes, even when you want to say no. Journal the question, "How does always saying yes impact my relationships? How does always saying yes impact my self-image?"

- **A**sk why? Journal the question, "Why do I believe I struggle with that habit? Am I afraid of people being mad at me or not accepting me?" Learn from your past and admit your responsibility to take ownership of your healing and personal growth.

- **A**pply your vision: How would you like to be in relationships? Visualize yourself saying no when it's necessary and begin to practice saying no and meaning it.

THE *I'M AN EXCELLENT PROBLEM SOLVER AND PERFECTIONIST* PERSONALITY

As a perfectionist, you are very particular about fixing everything and everyone in your life. You have an idea of what a perfect life and relationship is to you. You may come across as perfect in the beginning of a relationship, but you often push others away with your expectations of perfection. You try to fix them, fix their problems. As a perfectionist you struggle to relax and be yourself because you believe you must be perfect. Being authentic and transparent with others feels impossible, which is a major reason you find it challenging to have deep connections. No one is perfect, and you know that truth as you're reminded of imperfection the more you strive to be perfect. Perfectionists are hardwired to identify flaws in others and often magnify those flaws both in themselves and in the people around them.

The following is *the triple-A technique plan* journal of a perfectionist:

- **A**cknowledge—*"I struggle with always wanting to be perfect. I take longer to complete work projects and meet deadlines because everything I do never seems good enough. It's very difficult to engage in new relationships because I'm often so paranoid about what the other person is thinking about me. I almost never feel good enough."*

- **A**sk why?—*"I noticed I started struggling with being a perfectionist after going through depression in middle school. I gained weight, started struggling with my grades and didn't receive as much support and understanding from my mom. I started being hard on myself to perform better. After losing weight and getting good grades, I noticed people treated me better, so I began to challenge myself to be better all the time and strive for perfection. Now it's causing so much stress and failure in my relationships because it's difficult to connect to people."*

♦ **A**pply your vision—*"I envision myself enjoying happy healthy relationships free of anxiety and pressure. I desire to feel the freedom of being my authentic self and allowing others to connect with my unique personality. I envision a healthier carefree life and the enjoyment of strong relationships. I am committed to practicing my affirmation "I am enough" and I am working to gain a better understanding that I don't have to be perfect."*

THE *I'M YOUR NUMBER-ONE HELPER, SO YOU CAN RELY ON ME ALWAYS* PERSONALITY

You need to be needed, and it's hurting your relationships. You consistently attract needy people who are never satisfied with what you give. They demand so much of you that you often find yourself feeling depleted and unworthy. You struggle with this characteristic because helping others gives you a temporary sense of worthiness and value. You must understand you are worthy and valuable whether you're helping others or not. Learning to connect more with yourself and understanding the true value within you will help maintain healthier relationships.

If you struggle with *The I'm your number-one helper, so you can rely on me always personality*, you can substitute the habit of seeking to be needed through external validation by implementing *the love habit technique*. This technique is the foundation for loving and accepting yourself unconditionally first. Complete the following steps to connect more with yourself and implement *the love habit technique* using the LOVE acronym:

◆ **L**earn: Listen to your body daily and learn your physical, mental, and emotional needs. Study yourself and learn about your mind, body, and spirit. Ask yourself, Am I receiving love and acceptance within myself? What are the emotions I'm feeling, and what emotions do I desire to experience?

◆ **O**ptimize: Optimize your physical, mental, and emotional needs by accepting them fully and intentionally nurturing them. Optimizing techniques like meditation, exercise, and gratitude mindset journaling are shared in more detail throughout the book. Building a healthy relationship with yourself by accepting and nurturing your unwanted and wanted habits is the beginning of a healthy relationship with yourself and others. What are the relationships and habitual patterns you need to let go of? A major part of optimizing is letting go of the old to embrace what's new. What are the negative habits you need to change? How will you express love towards yourself during this process?

◆ **V**alidate: Validate yourself. Even if you don't fully believe or feel it yet, affirm that you are enough. Recognize the areas in your life when you sought validation from others. Ask yourself, How can I give myself validation today? It's also important to understand the areas in your life that reinforce the message and belief that you are not enough. Is that message reinforced at work, at church, or at home?

♦ **E**xperience: Practice and affirm feelings of love, acceptance, and validation as you love on yourself. As you take practical steps to care for your mind, body, and spirit, and take action to enhance your career and finances, you are reinforcing the experience you desire. Become intentional about being nicer to yourself and experiencing self-acceptance. Your happiness starts with you. External change doesn't create happiness. Happiness is a result of internal love and acceptance.

THE *I'M AN OVERACHIEVER, SO I CAN MAKE ANYTHING WORK* PERSONALITY

You find your value in your accomplishments, and you often get recognition from them. You may attract relationships with people who only want to be around you when you are succeeding. You may also attract people who are dissatisfied with your achievements, and because overachieving is a huge part of your personality, you strive harder to achieve and gain the validation of others. However, these types of people often leave your life when you go through struggling times. They don't recognize you beyond your success, mainly because you have defined yourself and built your reputation based on what you've achieved instead of who you are beyond accomplished success. Can you be great with or without achieving something?

Here's an example of implementing *the love habit technique* using the following LOVE acronym:

Learn: Listen and learn to identify personal goals, feelings, passions, and hurt. Do you feel numb, bored, or stressed in your body when you're not achieving? Ask yourself, Am I overachieving because I am seeking love, acceptance, or validation from others? How can I give my mind, body, and spirit what I'm lacking? How can I begin to serve what best for me above achieving solely for the recognition of others?

Optimize: Ask yourself, What are the unwanted habits that result from overachieving? Does it cause anxiety, stress, or exhaustion? How will you express love towards your mind, body, and spirit to eliminate the stress and anxiety of being an overachiever?

Validate: Validate yourself. Even if you don't fully believe it yet, affirm that you are enough. Recognize the areas in your life when you sought validation from others. Ask yourself, Why do I seek validation, and how can I give it to myself?

Experience: Practice feeling the feelings of love, acceptance, and validation as you love on yourself. Become intentional about being nicer to yourself and experiencing the feelings of acceptance. Your happiness starts with you. External achievements don't create happiness. Happiness is a result of internal love and acceptance.

THE *I'M LOYAL AND COMMITTED NO MATTER WHAT* PERSONALITY

Some may call you "ride or die" because you will stick through your relationships no matter what. You are loyal and committed even when others do wrong to you. You hold on to toxic relationships. Toxic family members get away with mistreating you because you are loyal. Your loyalty to others is also your protection from the fear of being alone. A desire for solid relationships is essential to the person who commits fully in all their relationships. Loyalty is your strategy to maintain relationships. At times you can seem to be too desperate. When most people walk away and leave a negative relationship, you may be the person who clings to it. The desire to never be alone, and the fear that creates, drives many of you. However, it can also leave you feeling empty, disrespected, and rejected.

The following is *the love habit technique* journal of an *I'm loyal and committed no matter what* personality:

Learn: *"I have feelings of anxiety in my chest area due to the pain and disappointment I feel from the betrayal of a friend. It hurts because I'm so loyal and committed to our friendship even though she has done me wrong several times. I've finally gained the awareness that I've been seeking love in all the wrong places."*

Optimize: *"I am making the decision to commit more to my personal well-being and to become loyal to my self-care. I am dedicating time to nurture myself through journaling and gaining more awareness of my emotional pain each day."*

Validate: *"I am committed to validating myself by honoring my body, listening to my inner voice, and implementing healthy boundaries when dealing with toxic relationships. I am loyal to the health of my mind, body, and spirit."*

Experience: *"As a result of implementing healthy boundaries, I'm experiencing more positive emotions including acceptance and love, which enhance my relationships with others. I am experiencing more love and acceptance as I give it to myself."*

THE *I'M A PEACEMAKER* PERSONALITY

You are fearful of conflict, so you obsess over keeping the peace. You avoid all confrontation. The people you engage in your relationships with are aware of your passive avoidance of conflict, and they take advantage of it. They know you ignore and dodge disagreements. You would rather keep the peace, ignore the issue, and move on or try to work things out in a calm matter. While there's nothing wrong with being a peacemaker, when you find yourself in a conflicted situation, it's healthy to engage in communication to work through disagreements. Pretending nothing is wrong is called avoidance, and there are consequences for living your life in avoidance. Use both *the triple-A technique plan* and *the love habit journaling techniques* to learn how to connect more with yourself and tackle the emotional issues that interfere with healthy communication.

HOW YOU MIGHT BE SABOTAGING WHAT YOU DESIRE

Now that we've explored the personality habits that negatively impact relationships, let's go into how you can subconsciously invite toxic relationships and sabotage what you really desire.

Unlike the way you see yourself (as simply going through highs and lows during various times in your life), most people are judging you by how you show up in the world from an outsider's perspective. Let's say you're going through a transitional season in your life, and you really want new friends. You make a new friend, and you express to them how much you're willing to help them with some of their busy tasks. You volunteer to babysit for them and even run errands. However, they start asking more of you, and instead of babysitting one night a week, they want you to pick up their child every day after school. That's a lot for you to commit to, but instead of saying no, you want to show your new friend that you're nonconfrontational, nice, and generous, and you end up feeling depleted.

Eventually, you start feeling as though this friend is using you. You are subconsciously unaware that you taught your friend how to treat you. In other words, you taught them to rely on you and expect massive service and generosity. The habits you've come to associate with your personality sabotaged your desire to have and maintain deep connections in your new friendship. Instead of enjoying a fun, compatible friendship, you only added more work and overwhelming service to your life. Your intention was friendship, but their intention was utilizing your offered service for the help they needed. While babysitting may seem wonderful for your friend, you can end up feeling exhausted, rundown, and resentful. Most people get mad at the friend when they are the one who taught the friend how to treat them in the first place. They manifested a *taker* as a friend.

Most people would blame the friend for being a user, narcissist, and manipulator without evaluating the major role they played in inviting the treatment. The extreme desperation for friendship and massive generosity led to depletion and attracted the undesired treatment. The truth is your need to be needed, which stems from insecurity, led to the user behavior in your friend. Although full transformation of personality habits requires a daily practice of awareness, having a vision, learning, optimizing, validating yourself, and experiencing what's working now, change is not a quick fix. You can't just believe or examine your way into permanent change, but it does help to have a daily awareness and a self-care practice to lead to positive transformation.

THE SOLUTION: POSITIVE PERSONALITY TRAITS TO STRIVE FOR

The following descriptions are of traits and personalities that serve you and your relationships in a more fulfilling way. These characteristic behaviors represent personal security and stability. They are traits of confident people who have a strong, firm self-image and high self-esteem. These characteristics teach people to respect and honor you.

1. The "My time and attention are valuable" personality
2. The "I am bold enough to say no" personality
3. The "I value focus and clarity; I stay away from confusion" personality
4. The "I prioritize myself first" personality
5. The "I'm worthy of good things" personality
6. The "I'm good at loving you from a distance" personality
7. The "I can be calm while having a hard conversation" personality

Let's go into each of these so you truly understand what they are and how harnessing them can have a positive impact on your relationships.

THE *MY TIME AND ATTENTION ARE VALUABLE* PERSONALITY

You are happy with your life. You have goals and aspirations that are very important to you, and you understand the significance of prioritizing your time. You are also aware of the power of your attention and energy. You can't afford to waste time on unnecessary drama and gossip, and people are aware of your energy and don't feel comfortable engaging in those low-level conversations. You are focused and driven about your dreams, and you don't waste time on negative small talk.

THE *I AM BOLD ENOUGH TO SAY NO* PERSONALITY

You are comfortable with yourself. You know what you want in life, and you are consistent with your goals. You plan your schedule in advance, and you rarely engage in idle time. You enjoy down time when you are doing things that relax and excite you. However, you are very clear about what you will and won't do. Therefore, saying no comes easy to you. You are confident and bold about saying no when it's necessary, yet it doesn't come across as being rude. People understand you are certain about what you are willing to do, and they respect that about you.

THE *I VALUE FOCUS AND CLARITY; I STAY AWAY FROM CONFUSION* PERSONALITY

Unlike the *problem solver and perfectionist* personality, you don't feel the need to fix everything and everyone. You are very focused and clear about what you want in your life and in your relationships. You are also intentional and straightforward about what's best for you. You don't feel the need to force connection. You know how to quickly determine if something or someone is a good fit, and if not, you allow it to be what it is. You never find yourself in complicated or confusing relationships because you value simplicity and ease.

THE *I PRIORITIZE MYSELF FIRST* PERSONALITY

"Who will take care of me if I'm always taking care of everyone else?" This is the question that the person who prioritizes themselves asks consistently. If you're not healthy, happy, and whole, how can you give all those things to another person? You understand you can't pour from an empty cup, so how can you expect to give of yourself when you're depleted? You happily put yourself first, and this is what keeps you happy and fulfilled. You are not ashamed or afraid to prioritize yourself. People don't always understand you or believe the same things as you do, but they respect you. They know they can't pull one over on you, and users avoid relationships with you.

THE *I'M WORTHY OF GOOD THINGS* PERSONALITY

Unlike the overachiever personality that will struggle to accomplish and make anything work, you know your worth. You don't get your value from accomplishments. When things don't work out, you lose a job, or you have failure in your finances or struggles in your relationships, you hold on to your value. You may feel sad and go through emotional challenges, but you never believe you aren't worthy of good things. You aren't defined by achievements but by your pure resilient soul. You can go through ups and downs and come out stronger and more refined. You gain value from others not because of your achievement but because of your confidence and strong state of mind.

THE *I'M GOOD AT LOVING YOU FROM A DISTANCE* PERSONALITY

You don't cling to unhealthy relationships. Protecting your peace and guarding your heart are core values for you. You don't mind distancing yourself from unwanted relationships. People understand your tolerance, and they know you will remove yourself with no problem. You have a powerful way of being kind yet distant. You are good at protecting yourself from unwanted toxic relationships. Others recognize your strength to limit your time and attention when it's necessary, and if they value having you in their life, they will level up to treat you differently.

THE *I CAN BE CALM WHILE HAVING A HARD CONVERSATION* PERSONALITY

Having peace and calm is very important to you; however, you are nothing like the peacemaker personality. You don't believe in avoiding all conflict. You understand there are some things you don't react to because it doesn't serve you to give it your energy. Nevertheless, there are difficult conversations that need to be addressed, and you are willing to engage in a calm, healthy manner. You are a strong and confident individual, and you know what you want; therefore, you can properly communicate and listen to understand. Because of this, people know they can't pull one over on you, and they will adjust to connecting in a healthier way or moving out of your life.

After reviewing both the negative and positive personality habits, you may find some that you relate to or maybe you would like to work on improving them. Allow the techniques in this chapter to be your guide in eliminating any negative habits. The positive personality habits not only strengthen and enhance healthier relationships, but they also eliminate negative toxic relationships. These characteristic habits can't be acted out, and there's no quick fix. There's no way to fake it until you make it. It requires a daily commitment to true mental, emotional, and physical change.

Now that you're aware of the ways in which you might be attracting toxic relationships in your life, let's learn more about tools related to self-validation, which will help you shift away from negative patterns. In the next chapter, you'll be learning more about the thoughts that help to create positive habits for better relationships as well. The goal is to always strive to move forward in a healthier way.

2 | COMPLETELY REINVENTING YOURSELF

You've done the tough work of looking at yourself in a new way and learning how your personality habits may attract unhealthy relationships. Now it's time to lovingly release those old patterns that have been holding you back from positive and healthy connections. This healing process is not just about healthier relationships with others but also having a healthier relationship with yourself. As you identify your unwanted habits and tendencies, it may lead to feelings of guilt and self-judgment. Judging yourself for being a perfectionist or codependent can cause you to feel worse; it can also interfere with positive thoughts that lead to positive habits.

Throughout this process it's very important that you are patient with yourself. Forgiveness is the key to healing the heart. Trauma, guilt, and shame will block you from letting love in. It's wonderful to work on forgiving others, but don't ignore your negative default thinking that hinders the forgiveness of yourself. You can make the choice to either follow thoughts of fear, shame, guilt, or paranoia, or you can choose to follow the thoughts of love, compassion, forgiveness, and faith.

The following approach, including the techniques at the end of this chapter, will help you create a strong self-image to automatically reflect these positive personality habits in your relationships.

MAKE YOUR HEALTH A PRIORITY

It is only when you first fully accept and prioritize a healthy mind, body, and spirit for yourself that you can radiate joy and attract healthy relationships. This is important because we teach people how to treat us by how we value and treat ourselves first. The codependent mindset assumes the role of "the fixer/the giver," often giving of yourself fully to another person while forgetting your own needs. This habit leads to obsessing over fixing the life of another person while neglecting your own. I often fell into this pattern as a wife and mom. When I started prioritizing myself, only then did I begin to experience a major difference in the way people treated me. People began to show me so much love, honor, respect, and appreciation. I learned that my daily habits influenced the quality of my life. These habits consisted of the first sixty minutes of my day. My morning routine includes five minutes of gratitude journaling, ten minutes of mediation, ten minutes of saying or listening to affirmations or a motivational message (detailed meditation and affirmation technique is shared at the end of this chapter), and thirty-five minutes of exercise, which consist of a mixture of cardio and strength training. This simple consistent habit of nurturing my mind, body, and spirit led to a happier life and healthier relationships.

COMMIT TO A DAILY SELF-CARE ROUTINE

Your personal happiness is based on you and only you. If you ever want to predict the quality of your future relationships, you need to become more aware of your daily self-care commitment. It's your consistent choices that gradually influence your self-image, which then influences your relationships. Ultimately, we teach people how to treat us. It's important to understand that you are responsible for your happiness, fitness, and emotional health. Instead of seeking happiness from others, create daily habits that contribute to your overall happiness. For example, speaking positive affirmations, listening to motivational podcasts, and journaling can contribute to your emotional health. Often societal norms and expectations condition us to seek happiness in jobs, money, relationships, and material possessions. However, you can create a lifestyle of self-care that boosts your internal well-being, self-image, and confidence, which will also influence the quality of your relationships.

REINVENT YOURSELF

To enjoy new success, new joy, and new opportunities, you must be willing to let go of the habits of the old identity and reinvent yourself. This process requires you to be open to doing some uncomfortable things that you have been avoiding. It may require you to leave your current job and commit yourself completely to a new career; you may have to let go of a painful relationship or go through a divorce. This process requires you to let go of old beliefs that are keeping you stuck in the same devastating situation.

UNDERSTAND YOUR SELF-CONCEPT

You perceive yourself differently than how others view you. Your image of yourself is based on your experiences and your behavior from past events. However, other people have a much different viewpoint of who you are, and whether you are aware of it or not, you are teaching them how to treat you. According to Mark Leary, professor of psychology at Wake Forest University, "You filter the cues that you get from others through your self-concept." Your idea of what people think about you is based on your own beliefs about who you are. However, other people are perceiving you in an entirely different way. It's those things you don't see about yourself that's giving people data and assumptions about you. Others are perceiving you through subtle ways like body language, attitude, demeaner, outward behavior and moods, personality, and physical appearance. You may feel clueless as to why certain people are deceptive toward you. Why do some people devalue and disrespect you? Could it be that your self-concept is different from their view of you? Could you be perceiving yourself as a kind giver while others view you as a pushover?

You may be unaware of your slouching body language that is translating as low self-esteem to people who are in community with you. Maybe you're going through a challenging season in your life but still view yourself as confident and determined. It's likely that others may assume you are passive, and they can take advantage of you.

Think about that friend who repeats the same behavior, moving fast in new relationships without truly getting to know a person, leading to failed premature connections causing under-developed toxic relationship experiences. Whenever you try to share advice on how she can change through patience, she gets angry and upset with you. She has no true self-concept, and she's not open to constructive critique. She doesn't view her actions as the cause of her unhealthy relationship encounters. However, if she spent more time observing her actions and how they influence the reactions of others, she would better position herself for healthier relationships.

When you resist self-awareness and feedback from others and avoid your self-analysis, it often leads to a pattern of unwanted relationships as well as a lack of accountability. This may influence others to lie to you or avoid sharing honest advice because of the fear that the feedback may break you. This keeps you in the dark about your true self-concept, blinded to your mistakes, and confused about why you have relationship issues. Based on these examples, you can easily see how a lack of self-perception may lead to repeating the same sabotaging behaviors and experiencing the same negative situations repeatedly.

HOW ARE YOU TEACHING PEOPLE TO TREAT YOU?

According to marriage and family therapist Michael Morgan, teaching people how to treat us is a process that involves teaching them "what is acceptable and unacceptable. It is knowing what we need and want and being able to communicate it effectively to others." However, if your behavior and response to others consists of you allowing and settling for mistreatment, you are teaching others it's acceptable even if your words say differently. People are more aware of your expressions, energy, and body language than what you say. These subtleties are habitual, and you are probably performing them unknowingly. The subconscious is a powerful thing. You are likely unaware of the repeated gestures, signals, and signs you are giving off habitually.

Much of your interpersonal performance for other people comes from your childhood and how you were programmed in those early years: the emotions, personality descriptions, and behavior patterns your parents emphasized about you. Maybe they called you shy and quiet, or rude and obnoxious, so you believed them because they were the adults, the dominating figures in your life, and because of that you took on a role, a personality, an image to emphasize the beliefs, habits, and character that replicated who they said you were. The issue with this is that they labeled you based on a particular season in your life as if that was who you would always be. During that time, you may have appeared to be quiet and shy because you experienced trauma stemming from your parent's rage and arguments or because you were just more observant and aware of people, or you just didn't have much to say. Perhaps, as a child, people thought you were rude and obnoxious because you didn't want to play by the "rules" in class. You were so excited about life, play, and having fun that you didn't want to sit still, fold your hands, and be quiet or stop talking. Instead, you wanted to run, jump, and dance, but the adults gave you a label because of it. Therefore, you believed them, and you took on the belief that you are unstable, bad, rude, and disruptive. Feelings of insecurity, self-doubt, low self-esteem, and an inferior demeanor have shaped your entire life. The sum of your negative self-image has influenced you to habitually and subconsciously teach others how to treat you. But you are so much more than those childhood labels.

According to psychologist Haim Ginott, "Even in fun, labeling can be disabling." It can be damaging to a parent–child relationship throughout life; parents start to view their child solely according to the label. The truth is, no single word or label can describe anyone completely. We are progressively changing, developing, and growing. The labels that described a particular time in your life may no longer define who you are today. The damage of labeling will lead to personality habits that limit the positive progression in your life and relationships. Therefore, release those labels that no longer serve you or your relationships by expanding your mind to how you desire to be treated and embracing more positive habits that support that desire.

TOOLS TO HELP YOU MANAGE PERSONALITY HABITS

Now, let's go into how you can properly cope with your personality traits and attract the life and relationships you really desire. Many people believe they must cut off their feelings or change who they are in order to maintain healthy relationships. You are a caring person, and that doesn't need to change. However, there are healthier ways to care for, serve, and help others while strengthening your self-care and eliminating the triggers of guilt and anxiety.

Applying mindful acceptance

Let's say your brother is going through a very difficult time in his life, and he's very overwhelmed with stress from work and from his marriage. He consults with you about it, and you feel the emotional stress that he's dealing with. Instead of getting emotionally overwhelmed and worrying about how to fix his problems, stop and take a few deep breaths to ground yourself and release the stress energy. Breathwork is a powerful technique to releasing stress energy. I like to start by taking a deep breath through my nose, breathing in for 5 seconds, then I hold my breath for 5 seconds, and finally I exhale out of my mouth for 8 seconds. I repeat this at least three times or until I feel calm. After completing your breathing technique, get clear on the understanding that you can't help by getting stressed by the reactions of others, and taking on their overwhelming energy doesn't help either. Make peace that your presence is enough, and you don't have to take action or strive to fix something in order to help. You just being there is enough. You can be a listening ear, a shoulder to cry on, or a prayer partner. However, the care you offer to others should never deplete you. Make sure you have the energy and strength from building yourself up first before you exhaust yourself trying to help others.

Understand your emotional capacity

Being aware of your emotional efficiency is very important. It's vital to set limits for people and situations that may exhaust you. If you're already stressed due to a situation at work, scrolling the news or hanging out with a friend who enjoys talking about their struggling issues may not be the best way to spend your time. Instead, take a break by putting your phone on "do not disturb" and spend some time at home relaxing in a hot bubble bath. This is a great way to release the tension and stress while increasing your emotional capacity and expanding your energy. Stress can cause anxiety and tension in your body. However, allowing yourself to relax and unwind will build the energy for a more active mind and restored body. As you learn to listen to your body and be more in tune with your emotions, you can protect yourself from things that drain you emotionally.

Let go of worries

Empathic people often worry about others. They want to do something to fix the problems and issues of life. They are fixers and often place most of their energy on trying to solve problems. They worry often and fear things getting worse for themselves and others. These worries often result in important personal issues being ignored. They are too overwhelmed with the problems of others that they fail to address their own situation. This can be consuming and draining. Make the decision to stop worrying. Meditation is a great technique that helps to eliminate worrying and feelings of anxiety. Worrying often happens as a result of stressing over the unknown misfortunes of the future or replaying the disappointing moments of the past. However, meditation allows you to stop and appreciate the present moment. A simple way of meditating is sitting still with your eyes closed and observing each inhale and exhale as you breathe. This simple practice helps you to calm yourself and live in the peace and stillness of the moment. Understand that worrying doesn't serve you or others; allow life to be, and allow others to deal with their own situation.

We've discussed personality traits that reinforce unhealthy relationships and how to cope in a healthy way. Now, let's explore the beginning process to help you create your own daily self-care routine. It will also help you develop the confidence, positive self-image, and stability you desire to experience in your relationships. Implement *The love habit technique* using the LOVE acronym.

In this chapter we will explore the "L (Learn)" principal in the LOVE acronym.

Learn: Listen to your body daily and learn your physical, mental, and emotional needs. Study yourself and learn about your mind, body, and spirit. Ask yourself, Am I receiving love and acceptance within myself? What are the emotions I'm feeling, and what emotions do I desire to experience?

YOUR DAILY SELF-CARE TECHNIQUE

Step 1: The first step is to understand that you are responsible for your own life, including how you teach people to treat you. You are not at fault for their actions and what they do, but you *are* responsible for your communication and how you show up in relationships. This is an important step because if you do not eliminate blame, you will always be the victim.

Step 2: Next, you're going to evaluate your emotions. What are your current emotional thoughts, beliefs, and habits that you are displaying in your relationships? Are you feeling insecure, needy, desperate, fearful, or resentful? Write down your emotions.

♦ *Evaluate what's acceptable and unacceptable in your relationships.* Who do you want to be in your relationships? Identify the character traits you want to display at work, at home, and in your friendships.

♦ *Evaluate what you need and want from your relationships.* How do you want to be treated? What is your relationship needs at work, home and in family and friend connections?

Step 3: Write a list of boundaries that will support your relationship needs. Here is a more detailed example of what healthy boundaries look like.

Many people believe that they'll get more respect if they are stern, harsh, or strict. They may also believe that yelling and raising their voice will make the other person listen to them. Instead, these behaviors are often teaching people to ignore, disrespect, and avoid them. Creating boundaries by consistently practicing new daily self-care habits can transform your relationships for the better. The following are boundaries that empower healthy relationships:

♦ *Model the way you want to be treated.* If you want your coworkers to respect and treat you with admiration, show them respect by listening to their constructive feedback, repeating it back to them showing that it was heard, and acknowledge ways you can work together. Clearly communicate, respectfully showing appreciation of their advice; this creates a standard boundary of how you expect to be treated moving forward, and if you receive any negativity afterward you are committed to maintaining your state of peace and respect because you are not controlled emotionally by the response of others.

♦ *Reinforce action you appreciate.* After having a conversation with your significant other about speaking to you in a calm tone when engaging in a disagreement, the next time they are calm and respectful during an altercation, express your appreciation. Let them know that you notice that they maintain their calm tone throughout the exchange. You can reinforce that behavior by keeping your calm and appreciating their efforts.

Creating these boundaries that benefit you has less to do with forcing another person to change and more to do with becoming the changed person that has a more positive influence on your relationships. As you focus more on becoming the best version of yourself, your relationships will get better.

Step 4: Finally, you're going to use my *vision writing technique* to create the vision you desire to experience in your life and relationships. What do you want to be known for? What do you need to let go of? Follow the steps in the following vision writing technique:

1. After completing your daily self-care learning technique, write a list of positive beliefs, habits, and healthy

relationship experiences you want to attract. You may be seeking more relationships that support prioritizing your health first. These relationships involve people who appreciate your self-care technique and often enjoy participating in the meditation and exercise activities. You may also decide to connect with relationships with others who value growth and individuals who seek to be more of the best version of themselves.

2. Write a letter of acceptance to yourself and to people in your life. Allow yourself to be transparent and write out all your feelings both good and bad. Then write out the importance of why you chose to let go of the resentment and embrace acceptance. After you finish writing the letter, read it out loud either to yourself, a trusted friend, or your therapist. Allow yourself to feel the emotions and then release them. You can even implement the breath-work technique mentioned earlier in this chapter to help release any emotions that come up during this strategy.

3. Write a list of positive affirmations you want to use to encourage yourself and read them out loud. The following are examples of positive affirmations that help shift the personality traits in the previous chapter:

   ♦ I am aware of the power of my attention and energy. I only engage in quality, healthy conversations. I am focused and driven about my dreams.

- I am comfortable being myself. I know what I want in life, and I am focused on my goals. I plan my schedule in advance, and I value my life and my relationships.
- I happily put myself first, and this is what keeps me happy and fulfilled. I respect myself, and others respect me as well.
- I am worthy of good things. I am confident, and I have a strong, healthy mindset.

Speaking positive affirmations every day is the one habit that can enhance the process of building your higher-self character traits, and it can lead to the manifestation of healthy relationships. I recommend adding affirmations to your daily self-care habit routine. I record my affirmations and listen to them in the morning while I'm getting ready for the day. You can customize the way you implement them. Writing them on sticky notes and placing them on your mirror may be helpful. What's most important is making them a part of your daily habits.

Remember, it's your responsibility to develop the character habits of your higher self. Your higher self may be resilient, self-disciplined, self-prioritizing, bold, confident, kind, and humble. It's up to you to determine who you want to become.

All this advice on creating positive habits and implementing self-care techniques sounds great, but the real problem kicks in afterward, causing major anxiety and fear. This is what holds most people back from progressing forward. It's the need to belong.

Sometimes embracing your higher self can result in ending or changing relationships, leaving many with the question, "Should I stay, or should I go?"

In the next chapter, you'll learn how to be the best version of yourself while maintaining relationships you care about even if you have outgrown them.

3 | THE POWER OF NOT FITTING IN

"Sometimes the place you are used to is not the place you belong"

—from the film *The Queen of Katwe*

It hit me all at once. I was unhappy with my life. Who I wanted to be and the life I envisioned to live seemed too far from reality. I wanted to be fun, fit, energetic, adventurous, and happy, but at that time in my life, I felt hopeless. It felt like I was stuck in a life that fit the appearance of my material world but served as an ill-fitting home for my internal soul. I wanted more, I wanted change, and I needed transformation.

We as human beings are wired for change; however, our fears, uncertainties, and discontentment often interfere with life's necessary process of transformation. Our energy to force change manipulates and hinders the natural flow of the alignment of change. We are built with the ability to adapt to almost any situation. Our brains are designed to seek patterns, identify threats, and solve problems for us to thrive no matter where we find ourselves in life. While change is a major process in life, we often fail to acknowledge the required patience and growing pain of transformation. Growth often comes with loss. Before you can grow, you must first let go of the things that hinder your growth.

EVALUATE YOUR RELATIONSHIPS

Evaluating your relationships requires a letting go of the force and striving of change to embrace the allowing and receiving of what's to come. This process is outside of your comfort zone and into the unknown. It requires saying goodbye to your attachment of what was and freeing yourself to receive what's new.

The process often leads to a reevaluation of your current relationships. Relationships are expected to evolve just as life continues to evolve and change. The quality of our relationships with others has a major impact on the quality of our lives. We are naturally social creatures, and our connection with others impacts our growth process. However, it is not solely our relationships that create inner fulfilment; it is self-revelation and an internal shift that connects us with our highest potential. As easy as it is to look at how relationships have failed us in our life, we can blame our parents, our best friend, or our ex. The real healing and transformation will happen when we do the hard work of looking within ourselves and identifying how we block ourselves from growing due to our own internal struggles.

Yet instead of doing the necessary work of becoming aware of the pressure we feel and where it comes from, we are distracted by the lifestyle and behaviors we see in the people around us. Much of what we see in others can be inspiring, but we can also limit ourselves to the capacity of what others have accomplished if we fail to discover our highest potential.

THE PRESSURE TO FIT IN

Could it be that much of the unfulfillment you feel in your life is a result of you subconsciously living your life in pursuit of what looks good externally? Are you living your life solely to "look" happy and successful? Do you struggle with the pressure to fit in to the traditions of your family and social norms of your friendships?

Striving to fit in and working hard to be accepted was a consistent goal in my early years. It started very early for me; as a child I worked hard for the validation and approval of others. My main intention was to do things to make my mom and dad proud. I didn't just want to make them proud—I also tried hard to make them happy. My parents were in a very toxic and abusive relationship. I witnessed their yelling, screaming, and verbal and physical fights. There was a pattern of police being called and me finding a place to hide. As a child I thought I could change their toxic situation by being very good and doing things to make them happy.

At age six I started cleaning the entire house while my mother was at work just to make her happy and to gain her acceptance and approval of me. At the time she didn't even know I could clean the house all by myself. She was surprised and very happy to come home to a clean house. I was the oldest, and I knew I was responsible for my siblings. I felt the pressure to perform well, be good, and make my mom proud. This was a heavy burden. The burden of fitting in and being accepted was also a struggle when developing friendships. I knew I didn't always fit in; I was different. That same year, at age six in first grade, I discovered my love for art after going to my favorite class, art. I didn't know it at the time, but art was my therapy. I could get lost in making art, it felt so good emotionally. I loved making art, but I could tell some of my classmates struggled in art class and didn't enjoy it as much as I did. My art teacher was so impressed with my artwork. She would hold my art up in front of the entire class to showcase what I did. I could feel the tension and the insecure energy of my classmates as they compared their artwork with mine. I was so uncomfortable with that attention. I just wanted to fit in and be accepted; I didn't want to experience the awkwardness of being different.

My childhood experiences led me to becoming the version of who I thought people wanted me to be. Instead of searching within and understanding who I was and what my soul desired, I focused on pursuing things that seemed more acceptable and awarded by others. This is what caused feelings of unhappiness and hopelessness. For years I lived my life desperately wanting to fit in and be accepted by others.

BELONG TO YOUR AUTHENTIC SELF

Author Brene Brown says, "Fitting in is becoming who you think you need to be in order to be accepted. Belonging is being your authentic self and knowing that no matter what happens, you belong to you."

Maybe you've experienced similar situations to mine. You tried so hard to get the acceptance and approval of your parents, and no matter what you did, it never felt like enough. Maybe you felt uncomfortable when you didn't fit in with other kids at school. Maybe you didn't have your own group of friends, or you may not be as close with your family members as you would like. You may not get invited to gatherings with your colleagues, or people may forget to include you in social occasions. There are times when you may feel as if people don't relate to you, and maybe that makes you worry or feel anxious in social environments. You may feel this way because you don't share some of the same interests and views. You may not agree with your family ideology or religious beliefs. Some people may consider you as different. Or deep down inside you know you don't fit in, but you hide your true feelings and beliefs because of the fear of not being accepted. There's a chance that if you are honest about yourself and your true feelings, people may reject you. All the rejection and lack of acceptance from others can cause you to hide your authenticity. Is it *really* safe to be your true self; is it acceptable to express your highest potential?

THE FEAR OF RELATIONSHIP CHANGE

Kim has a very close relationship with her mom. They talk on the phone every day; she goes to her mom's house several times a week to watch movies and eat dinner. Kim is now thirty-five years old, and she has a desire to get married and start a family. However, she doesn't have the time to date because after work she spends most of her time with her mom. Also, the thought of being in a committed relationship creates a fear of losing the close relationship with her mom. Kim struggles with the pressuring thought of, "How can I still be close to my mom while starting a new relationship?" Kim also feels guilty at the thought of limiting her time with her mom. However, Kim's mom has a husband and several children. Yet, she has placed unreasonable expectations on Kim to be there for her. Kim has dedicated her entire adult life to the relationship she has cultivated with her mom. Kim rarely makes time for her friends, and her relationship with her mom is her primary relationship. When Kim is asked about dating, she often complains about how it's so difficult to find a good partner, no one is serious on dating apps, and how she is fed up about the lack of faithful men. However, in reality, Kim is not fully committed to the dating process because she's more comfortable and committed to spending her time and attention on the relationship with her mom.

EMBRACE CHANGE

It is challenging to make peace with the possibility that evolving your life may lead to changes in some relationships. It requires a great desire to better yourself, a desire to embrace self-care, and self-acceptance before you can gain the strength to allow yourself to evolve regardless of how it may impact your relationships.

For years famous philosophers have been sharing quotes encouraging change. We are told to not fear change but embrace it. Change is often the answer to many life challenges.

Henry Ford said, "If you always do what you've always done, you'll always get what you've always got." American author and entrepreneur Jim Rohn said, "you can change all things for the better when you change yourself for the better."

We can all look at our lives and see things that should and could change, and this can be a positive solution, but change often means not fitting in, being rejected, and losing the acceptance of others. The feeling of failure is sometimes the cost of change.

Kacie was known as the fun, goofy, comedic, life-of-the-party overweight friend. She hung out with three other girls, Kelly, Janet, and Rose. They all enjoyed Friday night karaoke at the local bar, Saturday night girl talk pizza parties, and girls' trips in the summertime. Kacie understood that she was known to be the friend that made everyone laugh, she was expected to go out her way to appease others, and she had a history of failed relationships. Her friends often joked that she couldn't keep a man. She was also known as the friend who got rejected by the cute guys who were more interested in Kelly. Kacie was fed up and miserable with the way her life was going. She desperately wanted to lose weight, so she decided to change what she ate, she got a gym membership, and she hired a personal trainer. Kacie became committed to a new healthy lifestyle. When Kelly, Janet, and Rose called to invite Kacie to join them in their Saturday night girl talk pizza party, Kacie didn't attend. She was no longer interested in overeating, drinking, and being the goofy, comedic, life-of-the-party overweight friend. Kacie's new lifestyle change resulted in her building her self-esteem and self-confidence, losing fifty pounds, and meeting the love of her life, who later became her husband. For the first time in Kacie's life, she focused on her self-care, and she felt so happy and fulfilled. However, Kelly, Janet, and Rose no longer wanted to be friends with Kacie. They said she changed for the worse; they said she was selfish and arrogant. They vowed to never be her friend again. This was painfully hurtful to Kacie. She saw Kelly, Janet, and Rose as sisters. Losing her friends was heartbreaking, but this was the price of her change. She no longer fit in with her friendship group; although she felt sad and rejected, Kacie began to understand the power of not fitting in. Kacie's decision to change her lifestyle habits resulted in her loving and accepting herself more. The more her self-approval increased, the more the need for validation from others decreased. Kacie began to understand that the power of not fitting in has less to do with losing the acceptance of others and more to do with gaining the inner stability of fully accepting herself. She discovered that her self-acceptance, which came from within, was much more empowering than the validation and approval of others.

CONNECT TO YOUR INNER GUIDANCE

Today we are often so mesmerized by the allure of being liked and followed on social media. We went from living in a world that communicated to children, they should not talk to strangers, to living in a social media world where people do whatever it takes to fulfill the deep craving of attention and acceptance from strangers. Social media has become a platform for people to compete for external attention. This rat race struggle for attention has resulted in people no longer being in touch with their true desires but instead getting distracted by what looks good online. Becoming like the person with the most followers has become more appealing than going on a journey of self-discovery and following a path that's unique to your personal vision. This is where the true power is—you are much more powerful when you can build the inner foundation of self-care and emotional and mental stability from intentionally investing in your mind, body, and spirit. However, it's important to understand that as you choose to prioritize yourself, it may result in some people being disappointed.

Your family members may question your change and try to manipulate you into fitting into their view of you. Your spouse may reject the difference in you, and you may feel threatened that your transformation may result in losing your relationship. The tension from other people's opinion of you can cause the fear of change. This fear is what usually hinders people from continuing their journey of transformation. However, when you are seeking growth, enrichment, and life improvement, it's necessary to resist conforming to the old ways that no longer support you. As children we were conditioned to put lots of focus and trust on adult authority figures and other external things. In that process, it was reinforced to neglect our inner voice, emotional reactions, and spiritual intuitions. We were told to stop crying, be quiet, listen to our teachers, obey the adults, and be good, which translated to doing whatever the adults told you and you would be considered "good." When you were too loud, you were told to stop talking; this external persuasion led to a complete elimination of internally trusting yourself. This is the number one relationship issue, and the reason people struggle with trust. Trusting yourself first leads to developing a healthy level of trust for others. It's not that you don't want to trust in relationships, it's that you struggle to trust yourself to make the best decision for yourself because of the many years of being conditioned to neglect the internal essence of yourself.

The power of not fitting in has more to do with getting to a place where you no longer need to fit in and or need to be accepted by others because you have evolved to completely accept and trust yourself. This deep acceptance is a result of a culmination of beliefs in being enough because you belong to the internal love that lives within you.

There's a bible passage when Jesus was speaking to a woman who had lived her life seeking love in all the wrong places. She had many husbands, and after relationship after relationship, she failed to ever be satisfied with real internal love. During the conversation with the woman, Jesus begins to share how she could connect to an eternal life of fulfillment.

> "But whoever drinks of the water that I will give him shall never thirst; but the water that I will give him will become in him a well of water springing up to eternal life."
>
> –John 4:14

That scripture was not about drinking physical, tangible water; it is referring to an internal source that's unseen. It's an inner soul connection. It doesn't matter how many people you date, or how much money you make, or what church you attend, or what kind of house you have or car you drive, your fulfillment will never come from anything external. True fulfillment comes with the connection to your inner guidance and intuition that can't be given from external sources.

> ". . . the kingdom of God is within you."
>
> —Luke 17:21

For years I struggled with depression, low self-esteem, and unhappiness. I was working hard to be successful in my career, marriage, and as a mother. I worked hard so that I could afford my dream house, but nothing I did never seemed like enough. I had a belief that all my hard work would pay off one day and then I'd be happy. I thought the achievements and accomplishments would make me happy. But the more I strived to succeed, the more I felt depressed. It had gotten to the point of impacting my health. I experienced severe anxiety and panic attacks; I was gaining weight and experiencing shortness of breath. I knew I needed to change. I needed to make myself a priority. I started the journey of making a mental shift to no longer struggle to accomplish what looks good externally but to connect to my mind, body, and spirit by focusing on what feels good internally. I had to release the fear of rejection and the people pleasing habits and embrace what gave me inner peace and joy.

You may relate to me; maybe you've experienced seeking fulfillment, closure, or happiness from people, places, and things. As you shift your focus internally, you can connect with your inner voice, intuition, and internal guidance to lead you to fulfilment and joy that can't be found outside of yourself.

> "If prayer is you talking to God, then intuition is God talking to you."
>
> —Wayne Dyer

Fitting in and trying to be accepted can mean coping with the unhealthy behaviors of others and seeking approval and validation on how to live your life based on what's expected from those around you. However, applying the LOVE acronym to listen, optimize, validate, and experience assists you in self-discovery and connecting to the best decision for yourself. This allows you to connect with your authentic self and supports healthier relationships and stronger compatibility.

Learn: Listen to your body daily. As you continue your journey of growth, it's important to understand the challenges that occur in the relationships with those around you. Ask yourself, Am I feeling guilty because my friend said I changed, and I desire their approval?" Am I receiving the attention and acceptance I need within myself? Are there any uneasy feelings that I encounter when I'm interacting in a particular relationship?

Optimize: Optimize your physical, mental, and emotional needs by accepting them fully and intentionally nurturing them. Ask yourself, What techniques can I engage in that will benefit me during this season of my life? Will meditation, exercise, and gratitude mind-set journaling help to support me in the season? Building a healthy relationship with yourself by accepting and nurturing yourself fully is the beginning of a healthy relationship with yourself and others. What are the habitual patterns that can strengthen your intuition?

Validate: Validate yourself. Recognize the areas in your life when you sought validation from others by trying to fit in and be accepted. Ask yourself, How can I give myself validation today?

Experience: Envision your future ideal self and how you would like things to unfold in your life. Practice feeling the feelings of acceptance and validation for yourself. How would you like to engage in your relationships? How can you experience acceptance by accepting yourself?

YOUR DAILY SELF-CARE TECHNIQUE

Write a list of boundaries that will support your relationship needs. Instead of completely cutting people off and eliminating a relationship, would it help to create boundaries that limit the time you spend with individuals? There are relationships that you may value deeply, but it may not be helpful to spend a day or weekend with them. It may be healthier to spend an hour with them instead. Spending too much time with others may be overwhelming for you. Some relationships that are extremely negative may require you to apply the "No Contact or Small Distance Technique."

No contact may mean blocking their number and eliminating all contact while creating small distance and gradually implementing more space in the relationships. When implementing small distance, you may respond to text messages or phone calls a day later instead of replaying immediately. Allow yourself to become too busy to fully engage in an unhealthy relationship.

PART II

HABIT TECHNIQUES—THINK, BELIEVE, EXPECT, AND BECOME

4 | ELEVATE YOUR SELF-CONFIDENCE

The story in your head that you tell yourself about yourself becomes your self-image. Self-image can be defined as the way you see yourself internally and externally. It's how you think of yourself, what you believe you're capable of or not capable of, what you identify with in regard to how you contribute to your world. Your self-concept and personal beliefs about who you are create and shape your world. Your self-image constructs your self-worth and defines your personal boundaries and the quality of your relationships. According to writer and professor Suzaan Oltmann, there are three elements of a person's self-image: the way a person perceives or thinks about him- or herself, the way a person interprets other's perceptions (or what they think others think) of him- or herself, and the way a person would like to be (his or her ideal self). Whether you are thriving with a positive self-image or struggling to overcome a negative self-image, gaining self-awareness will empower you to enhance your personal and relational confidence.

If you currently see yourself as unattractive, unintelligent, undesirable, and/or unhealthy and if you believe that you are nowhere near the version of your ideal self, and if others perceive you as all of the above, chances are you struggle with a negative self-image. When a negative self-image becomes extreme, it can lead to comparing yourself to others. Some people struggle with hating their appearance or even seeking surgery and other risky alternatives to change their image. Other negative self-image coping behaviors can include avoiding mirrors and camouflaging your appearance with clothing, hats, makeup, and other material objects. According to *Psychology Today*, cosmetic procedures in the United States have dramatically increased over the last decade, with an estimated eighteen million people having undergone surgical procedures in 2018 alone. Studies show that the two primary reasons to seek cosmetic surgery are to raise self-esteem and improve self-image.

When your self-image suffers, you suffer, and your relationships will suffer as well. The good news is you can change a negative self-image by building self-confidence.

CONFIDENT HABITS

Confidence is not something that comes from avoiding negative thoughts and bad news. True self-confidence is built over time by taking action and facing issues head on. Confidence develops through consistent practical habits that cultivate a positive belief and trust in yourself. There are six habits that facilitate confidence and allow you to thrive as an authentic individual in addition to making a genuine impact in your relationships.

Confident Habits

1. Trusting yourself

2. Knowing and understanding yourself

3. Allowing yourself to be a beginner and trying new things

4. Taking action that supports your goals

5. Becoming comfortable with standing out and being different

6. Surrounding yourself with positive people, thereby eliminating gossip and toxic communication

TRUSTING YOURSELF

Real confidence is generated when you begin to trust yourself. As children we were conditioned to trust those who were in authority positions and follow them and listen to their advice. We developed a strong reliability and took on a firm belief from what the adults in our lives told us and taught us. In fact, trust plays a major role in the foundation of our family relationships, romantic relationships, and friendships. We even place a level of trust in social groups and strangers to a certain extent. We have trust in doctors who are strangers to us, and we trust our Uber drivers and even our airplane pilots without ever meeting them. Without fully being aware, we place a lot of trust and reliability on people we really don't know. Yet we are conditioned to struggle when it comes to trusting ourselves. We doubt our intuitive thoughts and emotional guidance. We ignore the subtle red flags and clues we feel internally, as if they mean nothing. However, to be a stable, confident individual, you must learn to trust yourself. You do this by creating the daily habits that support faith in yourself by trusting your inner voice, decisions, and overall loyalty to yourself. However, in order to trust yourself, you must first know yourself.

KNOWING AND UNDERSTANDING YOURSELF

Developing a relationship with yourself by listening to your wants, needs, and desires will build confidence. Years ago, I was asked, "What do you really enjoy doing outside of work?"

At the time work was a major passion in my life, and when I wasn't working, I was busy being a mom to my children and a wife to my husband. At that time, I didn't really have "me time" or give myself much opportunity to consider things that I enjoyed. I didn't make time to discover what made me happy outside of work and family. I felt like I lost myself and had become out of touch with knowing and understanding myself. I started taking time to listen to my inner voice and really get to know myself through journaling, hiking, walks in the park, and stopping to take notes on things that made me feel more peace and joy—that's when I grew to know myself. I had to first prioritize acknowledging my feelings, passions, and desires. When prioritizing myself became a daily habit, I grew to know myself. This practice enhanced my relationship with myself and built a strong foundation of self-trust.

ALLOWING YOURSELF TO TRY NEW THINGS

When you lack confidence, it will cause you to doubt yourself, avoid taking risks and trying new things, and procrastinate when important decisions need to be made. A lack of confidence can also cause you to hesitate on completing necessary tasks that create growth. People who lack self-confidence often limit themselves due to fear and low self-esteem. Starting something new can be risky and scary for anyone, and in order to grow and enhance your skills, you have to be brave enough to be a beginner. Every new job, new skill, new hobby, or new relationship will require you to be a beginner. However, some people struggle with the idea of being a beginner because being new at something will put you in the position of learning, which also includes failing. All beginners fail their way into experience. No one starts walking perfectly after taking their first step. There's a process of falling and getting up that creates good walking. Confident people aren't afraid of starting over and trying something new. They are brave enough to be a beginner when it leads to growth. However, people who lack this level of confidence will stay in unhealthy relationships for years, tolerate toxic jobs for decades, and allow themselves to be loyal to the disappointment of all to prevent failing in something new. It's the gut-wrenching fear of failure—however, confident people aren't afraid to pursue new things.

"If failure is not an option, neither is success."

—Seth Goldman

Confident people are comfortable with failure, because even though things don't always go as planned, they don't attach their image to failing situations. People often assume that confidence is related to success, but the truth is confidence is based on your relationship with failure. It's important to understand that you're not always going to win, but you can be confident in yourself regardless of the outcome of your results.

Rebecca was a full-time business owner of a retail company for nine years. Her business grew gradually throughout its start, and sales expanded tremendously in 2020 due to large traffic to her website and online shopping during the pandemic. Her business grew over 1,000 percent in one year, elevating her company to $1.5 million in sales. The fast growth led Rebecca to secure a larger space with a warehouse to manage the shipping demands. This caused her to sign a five-year lease, expand her staff, and purchase more inventory and equipment to handle the large increase of customers. Rebecca decided to take out business loans to help support the growth and cover the increase in overhead expenses. However, every month, bills were increasing, and within a year the money going out was much more than the money coming in. Her business went from having 50 percent profit margins to breaking even and eventually getting deeply in debt. The economic changes in the market led to lower market reach, which resulted in very low revenue and no profit. Rebecca was spending more than she brought in. This caused Rebecca lots of stress, anxiety, and shame. Her personal and business expenses were too much for her to afford. The business went from growing at 1,000 percent in 2020 to over $500 thousand in debt by 2022.

Rebecca did everything she could to save her business, but nothing was working, and after a creditor froze the primary income funds that kept her business going, she was forced to seek professional guidance. Rebecca was led to one option; she filed for bankruptcy. She was devastated, and her heart dropped at the thought of going bankrupt, but she moved forward. She owned that company for nine years, and she spent countless hours building, branding, marketing, and promoting her business. She was the face, the name, and the spokesperson for the business. Over the years she had gained customers, fans, partners, employees, and ambassadors who supported her and her business. What would they think? Who would she become? And how would she go on with life after ending something that was so close to her identity? The thought of filing bankruptcy and closing her business was painful, and it physically made her sick. Rebecca felt like she failed; she felt guilt, shame, and disappointment. The thought of filing bankruptcy was so stressful that Rebecca procrastinated and begin to avoid the thought of it. She tried to ignore bills, she avoided phone calls from creditors, and she eliminated all money conversations with her husband. But the more she avoided it, the heavier it felt, and the more she knew she needed to make a decision. Bills continued to add up, it became more and more difficult to take out loans, and she needed money for both her personal and business expenses. Rebecca reached out to me for advice, and I encouraged her to journal this one question, "How can I apply self-care to this situation?" Rebecca spent a few days thinking about how she could apply self-care to her life, and at first it led her to meditate and do things to strengthen her mental and emotional health. That led her to ask herself why she felt so much anxiety and stress, and she began to realize those painful emotions came from the fear of what other people would think about her. She wanted to free herself of the heavy baggage of financial debt and despair, but she was working so hard to hold everything together mainly to please others and maintain the identity of being a business owner. This led to the question, "How can I apply self-care to my finances?"

Rebecca knew then that filing bankruptcy, closing her business, and applying for a job was the best self-care decision and although it might cause others to question her, she knew it was the best decision for her mental, emotional, and physical health. After making that decision and consulting with her lawyer, she immediately felt the emotional and mental weight fall off her. Rebecca began to understand that as she stopped connecting her identity with owning that business and allowed herself to become comfortable with failure, she felt better. She understood that filing bankruptcy and closing her business did not define her. Her relationship with failure changed, and she freed herself from the guilt and shame for the business failure. Rebecca's confidence in herself grew as her relationship with failure and disappointment changed.

TAKING ACTION TO SUPPORT YOUR GOALS

Confidence is not something you have; it's something you do. There is a misconception that confidence is something that people have. No one is just born with confidence; it's something that's cultivated over time by taking action. It's like a muscle in the way that it's built over time from the consistent action that you've taken. No one is confident in the beginning stage of anything. A professional basketball player is more confident after taking the necessary action of practicing the sport for over fifteen years, shooting the ball in the hoop over a thousand times, and running back and forth, up and down the court hundreds of times. It's the years of taking action and doing something consistently that builds confidence. Building confidence in yourself results through persistently showing up for yourself every day. Confidence and trust in yourself are results of you consistently investing in yourself.

Personal confidence is strengthened when you prioritize your body by exercising, drinking water, and eating nutritious foods. You also gain self-confidence by habitually strengthening your mind when you take time out of your day to journal, meditate, and listen to positive messages and invest in your mental, physical, and emotional health. When you show up for yourself, prioritize yourself, and put your needs first—that's what builds self-confidence and even more importantly self-trust. You have to trust your intuition—trust the inner knowing and wisdom of your soul that whispers guidance through the various paths of your life.

Sometimes you will feel led to walk away from some situations and make tough decisions that may not make sense logically, but you have an inner knowing you must follow that can't be explained.

BECOMING COMFORTABLE STANDING OUT AND BEING DIFFERENT

Confidence requires you to be comfortable standing out and being uniquely different compared to the people around you. It's the courage to take ownership of your brilliance and not shy away from the attention it yields. There's something that successful people struggle with, after working hard, making sacrifices, and staying focused on achieving your goals. There's something unplanned that often happens once success is achieved—you hide it. Whether it's the deep-rooted imposter syndrome belief that you are unworthy or the fear of judgment from others, instead of proudly taking ownership of your success, you do everything to avoid the attention it brings. Could the diminishment of your accomplishments come from your upbringing where you were coached to be humble and quiet? Becoming a confident person will require the bravery of owning your success, progress, and achievements regardless of what others may think. This level of bravery demands a reinforced commitment to prioritizing your-self, which includes proudly shining a light on your accomplish-ments. The desire placed inside of you to achieve that goal motivated you to pursue it, which led to your accomplishment of it, which deserves celebration. Although humility is important, it requires confidence in order to achieve your goals. When you become certain and confident about the value you offer, you will see that value reflected in the way others perceive you. Hiding your success is a disservice to the world. When you develop the habit of celebrating yourself, you will eliminate the limiting beliefs that hinder your growth and future success. After celebrating yourself, begin to celebrate your success with your close inner circle of positive friends and family. This will enhance your confidence. Also, notice I said "positive" people. This leads me to the final habit of self-confidence.

SURROUNDING YOURSELF WITH POSITIVE PEOPLE ONLY, THEREBY ELIMINATING GOSSIP AND TOXIC COMMUNICATION

According to Northwestern Medicine psychologist and relationship expert Sheehan D. Fisher, PhD, "Social support is a very important part of being a human and therefore when social relationships break down or are damaged, it can have a big impact on our mental health and well-being." However, it's very important to not rely on one relationship to provide the majority of your needs. It's important to have healthy relationships in the areas of romance, friendships, and associates. A study on fostering healthy relationships by Harvard University shows that stressful interpersonal connections may lead to health problems such as heart disease. It's important to eliminate toxic relationship behaviors such as gossiping, arguing, yelling, and engaging in physical, verbal, and mental abuse. If you are currently in a toxic relationship with someone you care deeply about, it's important to begin setting boundaries. The purpose of establishing boundaries is to continue the relationship on healthier terms that support both of you. This reinforces you prioritizing your own well-being. Building self-confidence will require you to make tough decisions, and as difficult as it can be to create boundaries in the relationships that you care about the most, it will pay off in the happiness and success of your life.

As you apply the self-confidence techniques we discussed in the chapter, your thoughts, feelings, and expectations will evolve to impact your relationships. Learning to trust and understand yourself more, and taking action toward your goals, will empower your self-image and nurture their ideal self. This includes a daily practice of envisioning the best version of yourself. *What do you enjoy doing? What will make you proud of yourself? Who is your ideal self, and how do you show up in the world?*

Applying the LOVE acronym to listen, optimize, validate, and experience assists you in self-confidence and connecting to the best decision for yourself. Reflect on the following to guide the elevation of your self-confidence:

> **L**earn: Listen to your body daily. As you continue to enhance your self-confidence, it's important to understand the challenges that occur subconsciously in your mind. Ask yourself, What makes me happy? When I'm having fun and feeling confident, what am I doing? Ask

yourself, What can I do now to start taking action toward my goals? Why do I feel uncomfortable standing out or being different, and how can I overcome that feeling?

Optimize: Optimize your physical, mental, and emotional needs by accepting them fully and intentionally nurturing them. Ask yourself, What affirmations can I say and meditate on that can reinforce my confidence? Building a healthy relationship with yourself by accepting and nurturing yourself fully will enhance your self-confidence. What are the habitual patterns you can do daily to strengthen your self-confidence?

Validate: Validate yourself. Recognize the areas in your life where you are already confident. Ask yourself, How can I give myself validation today?

Experience: Envision yourself as the confident person you desire to be. Practice implementing activities that reinforce confidence such as exercising and speaking affirmations. What tasks will you complete to grow your confidence?

YOUR DAILY SELF-CARE TECHNIQUE

Write a list of activities that will support you in enhancing self-confidence. How can you change the story in your head that you tell yourself about yourself? What is the self-image you desire? How do you see yourself internally and externally? How do you think of yourself, and what do you believe you're capable of or not capable of? What do you identify with in regard to how you contribute to your world? Your self-concept and personal beliefs about who you are create and shape your world. Your self-image constructs your self-worth and defines your personal boundaries and the quality of your relationships. How do you perceive yourself? How do you believe others perceive you? How do you perceive your higher self (ideal self)?

5 | MASTERING YOUR EMOTIONS IN ROMANTIC RELATIONSHIPS

All romantic relationships are uniquely different, just as each individual is authentically unique, no one couple is like another, just as no one person is the same as another individual. We are all completely different, with various desires and needs, and this is what makes relationships complex. However, what's important is to have deep self-awareness and to understand that engaging in relationships requires your genuine acceptance of yourself and the other person in the relationship. The practice of self-care, not taking things personally, and not assuming things without the proper communication will go a long way in your romantic relationship. Having clear communication and expressing yourself authentically will enhance your connection to your partner.

While there are many types and styles of romantic relationships that work well for various people, it's beneficial to embrace what works best for you and your partner. As long as your relationship is healthy and free of abuse, you can uniquely thrive in a relationship style that works best for you and your partner. There's no one relationship type that works for everyone. There are several ways to overcome challenges, conflict, and miscommunication; however, it's important to connect with your partner on the type of relationship that's mutually beneficial for you both. Some people tolerate negative interactions better than others, and out of the eight relationship types I'm about to discuss, relationships that are considered to be "stuck" encounter the most stress, unhappiness, and depression.

Types of Romantic Relationships

1. Dating
2. Casual relationship
3. Situation-ship
4. Committed relationship/marriage
5. Stuck
6. Happy and independent
7. Happy and consolidated
8. Unstable

DATING

Romantic relationships that are considered as "dating" usually consist of two individuals who are spending quality time together. This type of couple enjoys going out together to connect and have fun enjoying each other's company, while also considering the possibility of a long-term future together. This stage of the relationship puts lots of focus on getting to know each other. This dating stage of a relationship can last as short as one day and as long as twelve years or more. Depending on the relationship goals and connection, two individuals may decide to make the "dating" stage of a romantic relationship long-term.

THE CASUAL RELATIONSHIP

The casual relationship has become more and more common in today's modern culture. With people avoiding long-term commitment, and many struggling to connect due to emotional unavailability, casual relationships are often preferred. These relationships are similar to the dating relationship; however, people engaged in casual relationships have no future expectations or long-term desires and are often open to explore dating other individuals. There are no emotional attachments involved. This is why it's very important to get clear on the expectations of the person you're in a relationship with; while you may desire a committed, long-term relationship in your future, your partner may only desire a casual relationship. This relationship can be painful when feelings evolve and one individual desires more while the other person is emotionally detached.

THE SITUATION-SHIP

This type of relationship is what many may consider complicated. The situation-ship is a combination of the qualities of dating, casual, and committed relationships. This relationship may consist of the couple living together and dating; however they don't have a label for their relationship, and they have no future plans of commitment. A situation-ship can be very draining and confusing for some individuals due to the non-label relationship status, the struggle to get clear on what the two individuals desire, and the fear of having the tough conversation of defining the relationship. Couples involved in a situation-ship often have more emotional feelings involved than a casual relationship while lacking the deeper connection and future plans of a committed relationship.

THE COMMITTED RELATIONSHIP/MARRIAGE

These are the relationships that are often glamorized in the media. It's the images of the beautiful clear water beach proposal engagement and the opulent celebrity wedding in Paris. It's the ideal of a dream relationship. Everyone is told to strive for this type of relationship. Often, if your relationship status is "in a relationship," you are mostly considered to be in a long-term committed relationship. When a couple has an understanding and agreement of being in a long-term relationship now and in the foreseeable future, that is considered a committed relationship. The titles of committed relationships include boyfriend, girlfriend, partner, husband, wife, or significant other. The next four relationship types are various styles that are also included in the committed relationship category.

STUCK

Although Hollywood has glamorized committed relationships as romantic fairytales, there are some long-term relationships that are unfulfilling, lack communication and intimacy, and may be unhealthy and full of conflict. This is the epitome of what I consider a "stuck" relationship. The *stuck* relationship often begins great. The early timeframe of the relationship can be considered as the good days; wonderful interactions and experiences are formed in the beginning. However, after some time of getting used to each other, the excitement fades and the relationship suffers as a result. Instead of discovering new ways to connect, grow, and rekindle the excitement, the couple feels stuck in an unsatisfying, dull relationship. Another example of being stuck is one individual desiring the end the marriage or break up, but they are delayed in ending it due to unplanned situations. For instance, if their partner begins to deal with an illness, the breakup is delayed to avoid the guilt of ending the relationship during a challenging time. However, ending a stuck relationship often takes encountering an exceptional event like infidelity or gradually building the momentum of an individual who's willing to make the drastic change in their life. However, there are couples who have been in a twenty-year stuck relationship.

HAPPY AND INDEPENDENT

The happy and independent couple enjoys each other; they are often supportive and share a warm connection. They have desires and plans for the foreseeable future, and they are comfortable in their committed relationship. Although they are in a happy and long-term relationship, they are not living together. They both have independent lives outside of the relationship, and that works great for them. This style of relationship is often common for younger adults who are completing college or focused on building their new career. As much as they enjoy their relationship, they also enjoy their independent ambitious lifestyle outside of the relationship. They can travel together or explore the world on a solo trip while maintaining a happy committed relationship.

HAPPY AND CONSOLIDATED

This relationship can be described as, "the happy couple joined together by the waist or connected by the hip." Unlike the "happy and independent couple," this couple does everything together. They spend most of their free time together; it's very rare for them to engage in activities apart from one another. They spend most of every waking hour in each other's presence. Some may consider this to be a codependent relationship, and although there's a great chance that this relationship can be considered as codependent, it's very challenging to label a wide range of relationships without knowing people individually. As happy as the couples are in this type of relationship, they are often faced with the fear of personal survival if the relationship ends. This type of relationship can also involve the blending of the two individual identities, causing individuals to question, "Who am I outside of the relationship?"

UNSTABLE

This relationship consists of passion, excitement, and warmth as well as heartbreak, disappointment, and emotional pain. In the unstable relationship, couples will experience cycles of breakups followed by makeups and the highs and lows of negative and passionate interactions. This type of relationship can be very addictive as couples are never bored in the relationship because of the high intensity of drama followed by a heightened desire and affection. This relationship works for people who thrive on the excitement of unpredictability, but it can be very unhealthy for many people, causing lots of stress, anxiety, and high and low levels of depression. This unstable relationship is not healthy in the long term and can create lasting emotional damage to an individual, creating a momentum of repeated toxic relationships.

SINGLE AND READY TO MINGLE

Whether you relate to the foregoing relationship types or you're single and not in a relationship, having a healthy view and understanding of relationships will help you gain clarity on what's best for you. Throughout my years of coaching thousands of people online, I've encountered two extreme mindsets of singles who desire to be in a relationship. One mindset is all about "getting ready," and the other mindset is committed to "waiting." The people who are focused on getting ready are very intense in taking action and consuming their time working on doing things to get ready for the relationship they desire. This includes going on multiple dates and signing up for several dating app subscriptions. These "getting ready" singles are very avid consumers of taking practical relationship advice, and they have a pattern of going from one relationship to another. They are known to always be in a relationship or on their way to another relationship. Many of them begin relationships deeply expressing emotional and physical affection, expecting for beginner relationships to progress quickly into long-term commitment.

On the other extreme there are individuals who vigorously believe that all good things come to those who wait. While that can be true to a certain extent, many singles with the "waiting" mindset find themselves waiting all their lives, to the point of losing the expectation of ever being in a relationship. The "waiting" singles don't actively go on dates; they don't express or represent their availability for a relationship. They fail to communicate the nonverbal clues of someone open and available for a relationship. Many times, people with the "waiting" mindset often appear to others as if they are already in a relationship by avoiding eye contact and all expressions of interest when encountering other singles. You will never catch this person flirting. They are very reserved, nonchalant, and sometimes bashful when it comes to entering a new relationship. They may deal with deep trust issues and the fear of failure when meeting someone new. The waiting mindset is often a result of protecting oneself from the unknown. Many singles with the "waiting" mindset would prefer dating someone more familiar whom they've known for years (such as old classmates from high school or a familiar friend of the family) than to date someone unknown. Although they may say they desire a relationship and would like to be in a healthy relationship in the foreseeable future, their behavior and mindset represent an individual who is comfortable and committed to the independent life of being single. They may not want to remain single, but their daily thoughts, behavior, and energetic vibe connect more with a single person's lifestyle. When they're asked about their relationship status, they have many excuses to why they are single, and one of the main reasons is, "I'm waiting on the right one." It's as if they believe the love of their life will knock on their door and then they'll live happily ever after.

A healthier approach to being single with the desire to be in a healthy, long-term committed relationship is to be neither "getting ready" or "waiting," but instead focusing on alignment. There are stages and phases in your life when you will not desire to date and other times when the desire, self-awareness, and intuitive motivation to be in a relationship aligns graciously in your life. Chasing dates, forcing connections, or being completely disconnected from others yet desiring a committed relationship all can be signs of a lack of alignment. It's important to get clear and align your life with the habits and values that reflect the relationship you desire.

THE RELATIONSHIP INVESTMENT

Don't just make a list of qualities you want to find in a partner; develop the qualities on that list. If you desire a partner who is physically fit, healthy, smart, financially stable, and adventurous, make sure you are actively taking care of your health and fitness, working on your financial management, and maintaining an active lifestyle of adventure. Become everything you desire in a partner. Look at the areas in your life you desire to improve and start proactively committing to your evolution. Having a happy and healthy relationship starts with two people who are committed to their individual well-being. Instead of seeking someone to make you happy or someone to rescue you from the pain and disappointment of failed relationships, understand that your relationship is not meant to complete you but to complement you. As you make your self-care a priority, your partner will witness the amazing life you have invested in, and the value you place upon yourself will speak volumes and impact the relationships you have.

Tracy was in a committed relationship with her boyfriend Steve for a little over a year when she found out that Steve had been spending time with Tracy's friend Sarah. Sarah and Tracy hadn't been as close as they were for a while. They went through a disagreement that led them to talking less and spending little to no time together. However, one day Sarah called Tracy and told her that she and Steve had been spending time together; he took her on a date, and he came to her house after their dinner date. Sarah sent Tracy screenshots of text messages from Steve. Tracy was devastated. All she could wonder is why Steve would do these things and not tell her. She trusted him, and that behavior seemed far from his character. Why would he do that to her? Tracy reached out to me for relationship advice. She felt betrayed and hurt. She didn't know what to do, and she needed guidance. I begin to talk to Tracy about alignment. I started by asking this question: "What of yourself do you see in Steve?" She thought for a while and then said, "I was happy when we were together; we enjoyed some of the same things, but the way he went behind my back and started dating my friend is beyond me. I could never do that to him or anyone. That is not a reflection of who I am." I explained to Tracy that based off what she had communicated, she was not aligned to Steve. His values, beliefs, and behaviors didn't reflect her high values of integrity and honesty. Although she had deep feelings and cared for Steve, they were not completely aligned, especially where it matters the most for her.

People often make the mistake of investing in a relationship based on how much they like a person. They focus on how much they like someone, and they make commitment investments; they think of how much fun they have with that person, and they make emotional investments; and then they think about how much time they've spent with that person, and they invest trust and hope in the relationship. Instead of investing in a person based on how much you like them, invest in them based on how much they are investing in you. Pay attention to the contribution they are making in your life. Great relationships are a result of two people consistently choosing each other. As wonderful as it feels being in a romantic relationship and enjoying the presence of someone who expresses desire for you, it's as important to guard your heart and clearly understand the foundation of the relationship. It's best to separate how you feel about someone from how they feel about you.

> "When people show you who they are, believe them the
> first time."
>
> —Dr. Maya Angelou

Never let your emotions blind you from the truth. When you are in a relationship, ask yourself, Are we investing in each other? We value what we invest in, and relationships often fail because people stop investing in them.

***

As you apply the techniques to master your emotions in romantic relationships we discussed in the chapter, you can align more with what you desire while guarding your heart. This will allow you to manage your emotions by prioritizing your values and no longer allowing your emotional feelings to make decisions in your life. This includes a daily practice of asking the right questions. *What of myself do I see in this person? What are the important relationship character values that enhance my life? What are the lessons to be learned from this relationship?*

✳✳✳

Applying the LOVE acronym to listen, optimize, validate, and experience assists you in mastering your emotions in romantic relationships. Reflect on the following:

Learn: Listen to your body daily. When you really like being in a relationship with a person, it's very easy to ignore the things you don't like and focus more on what you do like. However, your impulses and intuition will warn you of red flags and things that are suspicious. Listen to the warning signs.

Optimize: Optimize your physical, mental, and emotional needs. When you make a daily habit of investing in yourself—making the investments to ensure that you are mentally, emotionally, and physically healthy—this will allow you to maintain a healthy lifestyle that will welcome healthier relationships.

Validate: Validate yourself. Recognize the times when you have made healthy decisions in your relationships. Ask yourself, How can I give myself validation today?

Experience: Envision yourself in a healthy, happy, aligned relationship. What does it feel like to be in this type of relationship? Make sure you are gifting yourself the experience of a healthy relationship with yourself before expecting it from someone else.

YOUR DAILY SELF-CARE TECHNIQUE

Write a list of important qualities (e.g., honesty, loyalty, generous) you desire in a partner and then make it your priority to become everything on that list. This will allow you to align with what you desire. Then identify the negative emotional habits that resulted due to the betrayal of a past relationship, such as the fear of heartbreak, separation, or divorce. How can you begin to manage those emotions and develop healthier beliefs? When you analyze the alignment of the relationship by comparing your values with the value of your partner, this can help free you from toxic relationships with emotional vampires, narcissists, and cheaters while gaining more control over your own emotional landscape.

6 | PUT YOURSELF FIRST AT WORK

We tend to put our professional career and business goals in a separate box from our personal life. We are often reminded of the importance of having a healthy personal life and the value of eating balanced meals, exercising, and getting rest. However, many people struggle with understanding what a healthy professional life looks like. It's easy to get lost in the goals, projects, strategies, and guidance of colleagues, clients, and leaders of your organization, but in order to succeed at work, you must prioritize yourself. Having professional success is one factor, but the exceptional experience is enjoying mental, emotional, and physical health in addition to work success.

According to *Forbes*, one of the five essential habits of successful CEOs is that they prioritize themselves first. This is achieved by maintaining good health and work–life balance. These CEOs schedule their workouts, meals, and breaks for rest, and they block off time for family occasions like attending their children's activities. Not only do they protect their time on their calendar for important personal and family enrichment, but they also communicate why it's important to them with their staff, and they encourage their staff to do the same. Another personal priority task of top CEOs and executive leaders is to plan "think weeks" for strategic thinking, studying, and research. In the Netflix series *Inside Bill's Brain*, Bill Gates frequently planned mini solo retreats to read books and study multiple subjects in a Pacific Northwest cabin.

One of the reasons many successful professionals succeed is because they are healthy and happy. You will never see these people struggling, overwhelmed with exhaustion, grinding non-stop, and working around the clock. Excellent leaders understand the importance of brain capacity and sufficient rest. They must make important decisions; however, when you're overwhelmed with work and tired, you are more likely to make mistakes and struggle to solve problems.

✳✳✳

During the 2020 Olympics in Tokyo, the world's top gymnast at the time, Simone Biles Owens, withdrew from the women's all-around gymnastics final due to her mental health. Simone said the following words after withdrawing from the team final:

> I say put mental health first. Because if you don't, then you're not going to enjoy your sport and you're not going to succeed as much as you want to. So it's OK sometimes to even sit out the big competitions to focus on yourself, because

it shows how strong of a competitor and person you really are, rather than just battle through it.

—Simone Biles

What Simone Biles did was brave; while the entire world watched and the United States depended on her to bring an Olympic win, she made the decision to prioritize herself. With the pressures of sponsors and the entire world looking for her to perform, she was brave enough to put herself first, despite the hate and pressure from others to compete. Simone later stated that she was inspired by Olympian Naomi Osaka, who had withdrawn from the French Open and Wimbledon Championships earlier in 2020 for similar reasons.

The job of a professional athlete of an elite sport such as a gymnast comes with high levels of pressure, scrutiny, comparison, and perfectionism. It takes lots of courage to prioritize yourself in the mist of hundreds of millions of people watching. There were critics who said she should have been willing to sacrifice herself for the win and just do her job. The "just do your job" mindset is the reason people are stressed and overwhelmed with anxiety at work. It's important to take breaks, sick days and refuel mentally, emotionally, and physically. Just like taking care of your physical body is a lifelong responsibility, so is managing your mental health.

Almost everything will work again if you unplug it for a few minutes, including you.

— Anne Lamott

DON'T LET SOMEONE ELSE RUN YOUR SHOW

This is your life; you are the director of your life's show. Even in your career, you are the leader and CEO of your career. You must take ownership of your professional and personal life. Most people take ownership of their personal life but relinquish responsibility of their professional career to their manager, boss, or company's stakeholders. If your boss is unstable in strategy, planning, and implementation, constantly adding more tasks to your workload, you may find yourself stressed, confused, overwhelmed, and often times overworked. This can create chaos and disorder in the workplace. How can you focus on your professional growth and what matters to you if someone else is running your show? In order to take ownership of your career, you must prioritize your own goals and become proactive about your professional life by building a plan for your long-term success. It's important to build your own professional brand, focus on your own professional goals, and become intentional about your communication and the action you take.

Prioritizing yourself is also important for business owners and entrepreneurs. It's very common for an entrepreneur to pay themselves last and become personally depleted due to the habit of placing the business and clients first. According to a study by the National Institute of Mental Health, 72 percent of entrepreneurs are directly or indirectly affected by mental health issues compared to just 48 percent of non-entrepreneurs. As an entrepreneur, because you're the leader of your business it gives the impression that you're in charge of running your own show and no one else is in control. However, with business growth comes a demanding increase of customer service, and that's when clients gain control and hiring staff expands, and the larger the company grows the less control the entrepreneur has in the business. However, maintaining a mindset to prioritize your mental, emotional, and physical health is also very important as an entrepreneur. This can be very challenging while holding so much responsibility as a business owner.

INVEST IN YOUR PROFESSIONAL LIFE

Owning your career is consistently measuring yourself against your own progress and goals and taking full responsibility for your achievement and shortcomings. Taking ownership of your career allows you to go beyond the expectations set by your employer, customers, or colleagues. When you're proactive about your career, by setting goals, cultivating your professional brand, and progressively performing exceptionally, this creates an awareness of your value to your employer or business. This positions you to negotiate for promotions, salary increases, and benefits. You are positioned for growth. However, taking ownership of your career requires your investment in yourself. It's important to invest in your personal health, education growth, and traditional and nontraditional trainings in addition to the development of your skills. These are all essential to taking ownership of your career.

First, it's important to have a vision of the career your desire. What is the ultimate position or level of business you desire to have? What does your day-to-day work-life look like? What are the benefits that are important to you regarding this career, and why do you desire to acquire them? What can you begin to do to position yourself for this type of career? Once you have identified the steps needed to complete in order to have this type of career, begin the plan to make investments in yourself to support the vision of your desired career.

CREATE PROFESSIONAL BOUNDARIES

Creating healthy boundaries in the workplace is another way of prioritizing yourself. Protecting your time by blocking off time to complete top priorities first is a great way of setting boundaries. Internal meetings into which others may want to pull you will be secondary to your scheduled priority tasks. This will allow you to be more productive and goal-driven, and it gives you more control over your career. Creating healthy professional boundaries allow you to maintain structure and order in the workplace. These boundaries are a way for you to communicate to others what's important to you. If you create the boundary of not checking emails when you're on vacation, you are communicating to your coworkers that you are not available for work while you're on vacation. When working with people of various personalities and behaviors, it's important to communicate and clearly express the importance of maintaining healthy boundaries both verbally and nonverbally.

You owe it to yourself to protect your peace, and you should never feel guilty for creating healthy boundaries and guarding your heart. Real growth starts when you take ownership of your life and make the necessary changes that are best for you. It's important to understand that you have the power to change your life.

Speaking up for yourself and having direct communication in conversations and emails are also very important ways to implement your boundaries. There can be both a spoken and unspoken way of communicating your work relationship boundaries to eliminate pushover, rude, and insensitive behavior from others. When you become an advocate for yourself at work, it can help you prevent burnout by not overextending yourself to take on tasks that deplete you. This allows you to maintain a healthy work–life balance. It's also important to validate your own emotions and perspective instead of surpassing or avoiding your feelings.

According to a study by Gallup, 50 percent of employees resign from their job because of a bad relationship with their manager.

People leave managers, not companies.
—Marcus Buckingham

Whether you're communicating with your manager or coworker, it's important to confidently speak up and communicate clearly and directly with others. The mastery of direct and solution-focused communication allows you to focus on finding solutions to problems instead of judgment-focused communication, which shifts from solving the problem to placing more energy on judging the work or the person. This judgment-focused communication can come across as condescending and distract coworkers from finding solutions to problems; instead, they will find ways to either address the situation or avoid conflict.

PRACTICE EMOTIONAL INTELLIGENCE

Everyone wants to feel valued and needed, and it's important to communicate that in the workplace. Practicing emotional intelligence can allow you to properly manage conflict, connect, inspire, and influence others. One of the best ways to manage your emotions in the workplace is to remember to not take things personally. Miscommunication and a lack of understanding are very common when working with people of different personalities. Don't take it personally; the things people say and do create a projection of their reality. When you consistently remind yourself to not take things personally, this mindset will help you manage your emotions more effectively. The things that people say and do has more to do with what's going on with them and less to do with you, so don't take it personally. It's human nature to think that the things people do are because of you and something you've done. Instead of adapting to the energy that others give off, influence the environment with the energy you choose to maintain that supports you in a healthy way. You are responsible for how you feel and how you act, regardless of what someone else does. As you practice not taking things personally and not reacting to the vibes and energy of others, the things people say and do will not have much of an impact on you. Instead hold on to yourself—your own vibes, boundaries, and feelings—despite what others give off. We can't control others, but we can control ourselves and protect our peace by not adapting to their negative energy.

It's important to realize that you have so much control over your life when you practice self-discipline and self-awareness. You don't have to suffer and become overwhelmed with stress because of the action of others. You have the power to react in a way that supports you. You can choose to focus on the wonderful things in your life and give more energy and power to feeding desires and starving your distractions. However, when you allow yourself to dwell on issues with others and become upset, that doesn't serve you at all. Remind yourself of the power and control you have in your career, finances, and business. You can always choose how to respond and handle situations without allowing yourself to be offended by others. You can choose to always show up as your best self while maintaining the habit of prioritizing yourself both in your personal and professional life.

✳✳✳

As you apply the techniques to put yourself first at work, this will allow you to muster the courage to prioritize yourself even despite the difficulties you face in your career. In a society that has sold the idea of sacrificing yourself for others and insisting on the message of putting others first, we've all learned the detrimental effects this ideology has on our health. Now you understand that you can thrive at work while putting yourself first. Asking yourself the right questions will build self-trust and elevated confidence. *What is the ultimate position or level of business you desire to have? What does your day-to-day work life look like? What are the benefits that are important to you regarding this career, and why do you desire to acquire them? What can you begin to do to position yourself for this type of career?*

When applying the LOVE acronym to listen, optimize, validate, and experience to assist you in putting yourself first at work, reflect on the following:

> **L**earn: Listen to your body daily. While others may reinforce a message of "just do your job regardless of how you feel," listen to your mental, emotional, and physical warning signs. Are you feeling overwhelmed, depleted, or stressed? You may need to take some time off, talk with your therapist, get more rest, or begin a new career plan for a healthier work life.
>
> **O**ptimize: Optimize your work schedule by "time blocking" to gain more control over your work day and proactively set aside time for breaks, just to think, or to complete

important tasks that can get overlooked by distracting busywork.

Validate: Validate yourself. Take time to write out and keep track of your wins and become intentional about celebrating yourself. Don't wait for your boss and colleagues to acknowledge your success; create the habit of acknowledging yourself.

Experience: Reflect and emotionally experience the career and work life you desire. Feel the feelings of being in the high-level position. What does it feel like emotionally? What are the encounters you have with colleagues on that level?

YOUR DAILY SELF-CARE TECHNIQUE

Write a list of important qualities you desire in a successful career where your mental, emotional, and physical health is top priority. Then identify the positive emotional habits that resulted due to enjoying the work you do. When you analyze the alignment of the career you desire by comparing your daily habits, thoughts, beliefs, schedule and plans, you can begin to prepare yourself to receive that healthy career by committing yourself to it daily.

PART III

UNLOCKING YOUR DISCERNMENT— ALIGN, EXECUTE, AND IMPACT

7 | PROTECTION FROM DECEPTION AND MANIPULATION

After coaching hundreds of women online for over nine years, I decided to conduct my first case study by surveying more than seventy women who struggled with relationship issues. I discovered that the main reason over 80 percent of the women were fearful of engaging in a new relationship was due to their lack of character judgment. They didn't trust themselves to make the right decisions regarding relationships because of past relationship experiences that involved deception, infidelity, manipulation, and other toxic encounters. The momentum of deceptive and manipulative relationships creates behavior patterns that attract similar experiences in new relationships. The repetitive cycle of unhealthy relationships can lead one to believe that they are not good with relationships, gaining an identity of being a failure in relationships.

It's very common to get distracted by surface-level qualities of a person like their flattery, charisma, good looks, and charm. We make assumptions of what kind of person someone is by how they appear. However, you can't determine a person's character based on surface-level appearances. It's much easier for someone to hide their true intentions in the beginning of a relationship. That's why it's important to take your time to get to know a person deeply before developing a serious relationship.

***

Bridget was one of my clients who struggled with a lack of character judgment that led to an unhealthy relationship. She shared how she met John online after getting messages from him about how beautiful she looked in her recently posted vacation pictures from Cancun, Mexico. He also expressed how interested he was in meeting her in person. Soon after communicating online and talking on the phone for a week, Bridget and John scheduled some time to meet in person. Bridget had previously ended a six-year relationship, and John had also recently broken up with his fiancé. Bridget felt desperate to get her mind off her ex. She enjoyed spending time with John, going on dates, and enjoying his attention and affection. John lavished her with flowers and gifts; he called her every morning to have daily devotion over the phone, and he quickly made plans to one day marry her. John said everything Bridget wanted to hear. He did everything so right. Bridget's friend Kim expressed her concerns: "Something seems off with him—he doesn't seem genuine; he seems as if he's hiding something. I wouldn't trust him. It's like he's trying hard to be the perfect guy." Bridget ignored everything Kim had to say; she was falling in love with John, and things were moving fast. It had been four months, and Bridget discovered that she was pregnant with her first child, John's third child. Bridget never wanted to be a single parent, and because she was in love with John and wanted a family, they decided to plan the wedding to happen before the baby was born. Six months after the wedding and after their baby boy was born, Bridget found out that John had another baby by a different woman during the same time he was in a relationship with Bridget.

Bridget was devastated and heartbroken; she trusted John, and she wanted to make their marriage work despite the news. However, once the news of John's infidelity was revealed, John changed. He no longer wanted to be married, and he began mistreating Bridget. He tried to make her believe it was her fault that he cheated. He began leaving the house and not coming home for days. He started ignoring Bridget's phone calls and flirting with different women online. Bridget called her friend for support: "Kim, I don't know what to do, it's like he's a different person, I don't recognize him at all. He's not the person I met; he doesn't do all the wonderful things he did in the beginning. He's verbally abusive and manipulative. He neglects me and the baby, and he no longer want to be married." She was dealing with a lot, parenting the new baby, struggling with postpartum depression, and coping with John abandoning her. This was causing Bridget mental and emotional stress. She lost her appetite and began to feel sick and lose weight.

DECEPTION REVEALED

What Bridget didn't realize was that John didn't change; he just hid the sides of his character that he didn't want to reveal. In the beginning of their relationship John gave Bridget extreme attention and affection in an attempt to influence and manipulate her and to have dominant control in their relationship. He did this by calling several times a day, having daily devotional, giving her gifts every day, and making long-term commitments, like promising marriage in efforts to win her over in a short period of time. This manipulative strategy is called love bombing. According to *Psychology Today*, "love bombing is a pattern of overly affectionate behavior that typically occurs at the beginning of a relationship, in which one party bombs the other with an over-the-top display of adoration and attention. The love bombing behavior includes showering a person with gifts, and compliments, and persistently maintaining constant contact by spending increasing amounts of time together. Love bombing is a deliberate and manipulative strategy that's used in order to gain the upper hand over a new partner and to increase one's dependency on the bomber."

PRACTICE GOOD CHARACTER JUDGMENT

It's very common to struggle to properly judge a person's character because their surface expressions, gestures, and performance behavior can be a distraction. When a person is good looking, charming, and says everything you want to hear, it's easy to get mesmerized in their flattery while ignoring all the red flags. Once you make the mental decision that you really like them, that ideal image of who you believe them to be is reinforced in your view of them whether it's who they really are or not. Instead of developing an ideal belief of who you think a person is, do the following to determine a person's true character:

1. Be observant.
2. Study the extreme ways of a person.
3. Look at their patterns.
4. Pay attention to how they deal with uncertainty.

BE OBSERVANT

During the beginning stage of getting to know a person, it's very important to be observant and analyze who they are. We often get in the habit of overly emphasizing the behavior and habits we like from an individual while ignoring subtle warning signs that they reveal. While you may really like a person, it's important to also be very observant and take your time getting to know an individual. People are very complex, and they have different moods, expressions, and behaviors. As you become more observant by listening more and allowing them to talk, asking questions to build a deeper understanding of who they are and what their family is like, this will assist you in practicing good character judgment skills. As you are observant, it's also important that you take your time in building intimacy in the relationship. Developing connection with a new partner is a process and should not be rushed.

STUDY THE EXTREME WAYS OF A PERSON

Often when people are extreme in one area of their lives, it's usually because they are trying to hide another side of their personality. John showed extreme behavior in the very beginning of the relationship with Bridget. The love-bombing behavior of calling several times a day, giving flowers and other gifts every day, and consuming her time by always being around was all very extreme behavior. When a person is very extreme, that may be a sign that they're trying really hard to hide their true behavior, which may be the opposite of the overly positive character you're experiencing. This explains the abandonment and ghosting behavior of John toward the end of the relationship. You can study a person's extreme ways by observing, and by asking questions if it doesn't feel authentic and intentionally controlling yourself so that you do not become emotionally attached to their inner marketing department. Ask yourself, What could be behind this extreme behavior? How can I protect myself to not become so dependent on the person?

LOOK AT THEIR PATTERNS

If they talk bad and disrespect their ex, it's very likely that one day they may talk bad about you. A person's pattern will reveal their truth. If they have a pattern of disrespecting their mom or being late for dates and complaining or being rude to restaurant servers, those are red flags of someone with relationship issues. Don't ignore their patterns. People who are always late are revealing a pattern of pride and arrogance. Their pattern of tardiness may stem from a belief that their time is more important and it's acceptable for other people to wait for them. Could the person who always shows up late have feelings of entitlement? It's very common to overlook when the other person gets frustrated easily with waiters or servers at a restaurant. However, pay attention to any pattern of mistreatment they display toward another person, whether it's with family, strangers, or ex relationships. Those are signs of an individual's character. Never overlook the patterns of a person's character.

PAY ATTENTION TO HOW THEY DEAL WITH UNCERTAINTY

It's easy to have great character in the beginning of a relationship when everything is going great. However, a person's real character is revealed when they're faced with uncertainty. Pay attention how they handle situations that are out of their control. How do they react to stress at work? How do they deal with unexpected family drama, financial crisis, or life's uncertain situations? People have a very hard time hiding their true character when encountering uncertain circumstances in life. You can learn so much about a person when observing how they deal with tough times in their life. Do they become quieter and withdraw from social interaction? Do they express patience and express a level of faith and belief in their ability to overcome the situation?

YOU HAVE YOUR OWN PATTERNS

As important as it is to understand the patterns of the person you're in a relationship with, it's even more important to understand your own patterns. The more you understand yourself, the more you can make wise decisions on how to properly connect with others in a healthy relationship. Observe and analyze how you handle uncertainty in your life, and know your patterns when dealing with relationships with your family and friends. What are some of the extreme character traits you display in relationships? Are you clingy and extremely attached to a relationship, or are you emotionally unavailable and detached? Why do you react the way that you do, and how does your behavior impact your relationships? Instead of becoming a victim of toxic relationships and finding yourself doomed as a hopeless romantic, you can free yourself by taking responsibility for your own healing and growth. It's liberating to know that you can control your response and evolve yourself through the growth mindset of getting rid of the emotional baggage from past relationships. You no longer have to be the victim of a negative relationship, but you can now be the victor of your life.

To become enraged at a person's behavior is as foolish as to be angry with a stone because it rolls into your path bruising your foot. And the wisest thing you can do, is to make peace with those whom you cannot change.

—Authur Schopenhauer

People are like unpredictable stones that roll into your path; just like you wouldn't get angry with a stone that rolls in front of you, hitting your foot, the best thing to do is to adjust your awareness to respond in your favor if it happens again. It doesn't serve you to be angry when people clash with you. They are who they are; make the necessary adjustments to liberate and free yourself by not taking it personally. Complaining and blaming puts you at a disadvantage; it drains and consumes you, causing you to personalize the situation.

EQUIP YOURSELF TO HANDLE THE CHALLENGES

Life is not always easy; you will deal with resistance, and sometimes people may oppose you. It's important to take on the stance of a warrior. A warrior has the courage to protect themselves and develop the necessary skills to accomplish their goals. The stance of a warrior is calm and courageous. A warrior has the wisdom to protect their peace, guard their heart, and properly manage their emotions. A warrior's mindset understands that cutting ties with people who consistently hurt you isn't enough; you must also cut ties with the version of yourself who allowed the behavior to continue as long as it did. Real growth starts with taking ownership of your life. It's about eliminating the victim role and blaming others for your life results, and taking responsibility for your healing. When you keep your standards high, it protects you from settling for less and eliminates low-quality relationships. It takes courage to have high standards and to stick to them. It's important to focus on what's best for you, and only you can know what's best for you and what standards to set in your life.

THE GROWTH MINDSET

Your attitude is what determines your success in life and relationships. When you focus on obstacles, that challenge is magnified in the life you create. You are the influencer of how negative circumstances affect your life. According to Stanford psychologist Carol Dweck, a growth mindset is the belief that a person's capacities and talents can be improved over time. An individual who has a fixed mindset believes that his or her character traits are nearly impossible to change. They don't believe much in personal growth investments that enhance and develop a person's life. While it's helpful to understand deception and manipulation in efforts of protecting yourself and having healthy relationships, it's even more important to build yourself up mentally and emotionally to handle whatever comes your way. You can control any situation if you first control yourself; when you control yourself, it changes how you experience the situation. When you put your energy on things that are in your control and ignore what is not, you become empowered through focus and self-discipline. This is when you gain the results of the growth mindset. Toxic people cannot impact you; negative and narcissistic people have no control over you. You are no longer distracted by other people's opinions, feelings, or insults because your focus is only on what you can control. It takes a focused discipline of self-control to not take things personally. It requires you to strengthen your emotional resilience and develop a mindset prepared to deal with challenges by practicing emotional detachment from desired outcomes.

***

Now that you've gained the practical tools for building good judgment of character and creating habitual skills of self-discipline of self-control, you can now apply this knowledge when engaging in relationships. This includes a daily practice of not taking things personally, analyzing a person's extreme behavior, and emotionally detaching from a specific desired outcome. Start by asking yourself the following questions. *What are some of the extreme character traits you display in relationships? Are you clingy and extremely attached to a relationship, or are you emotionally unavailable and detached? Why do you react the way that you do, and how does your behavior impact your relationships?*

***

Applying the LOVE acronym to listen, optimize, validate, and experience assists you in building good judgment of character. Reflect on the following to guide your engagement in relationships.

Learn: It's very important to be observant and analyze who they are. We often get in the habit of overly emphasizing the behavior and habits we like from an individual while ignoring subtle warning signs that they reveal. While you may really like a person, it's important to also be very observant and take your time getting to know an individual. People are very complex, and they have different moods, expressions, and behaviors. As you become more observant by listening more and allowing them to talk, asking questions to build a deeper understanding of who they are and what their family is like, this will assist you in practicing good character judgment skills.

Optimize: Ask yourself, How can I be more observant in my relationships? You can study a person's extreme ways by observing them, asking questions if they don't feel authentic, and if they have controlling behavior, protect yourself from becoming emotionally attached to them. Ask yourself, What could be behind this extreme behavior? How can I protect myself from becoming so dependent on the person?

Validate: Validate yourself. Recognize the areas in your life where you are already practicing self-control and discipline. Ask yourself, How can I give myself validation today?

Experience: Envision yourself with the growth mindset of a warrior. It's important to take on the stance of a warrior. A warrior has the courage to protect themselves and develop the necessary skills to accomplish their goals. The stance of a warrior is calm and courageous. A warrior has the wisdom to protect their peace, guard their heart, and properly manage their emotions. A warrior's mindset understands that cutting ties with people who consistently hurt you isn't enough; you must also cut ties with the version of yourself who allowed the behavior to continue as long as it did.

YOUR JUDGMENT OF CHARACTER TECHNIQUE

As you implement the techniques listed in this chapter to be observant, study the extreme ways of a person, look at their patterns, and pay attention to how they handle uncertainty, you will be able to maintain a good judgment of character, which will assist you in eliminating all deceptive and manipulative relationships. Pay attention to how a person handles situations that are out of their control. How do they react to stress at work? How do they deal with unexpected family drama, financial crisis, or life's uncertain situations? People have a very hard time hiding their true character when encountering uncertain circumstances in life. You can learn so much about a person when observing how they deal with tough times in their life. Do they become quieter and withdraw from social interaction? Do they express patience, and express a level of faith and belief in their ability to overcome the situation?

8 | SECRET HABITS OF HAPPINESS

It was one of the darkest seasons of my life, yet it became one of the most inspiring times, leading to my commitment to a life-changing practice of habits of happiness. In that dark season I was depressed, stress, worried, and exhausted. I had insomnia, anxiety, and panic attacks, and I was dealing with physical health issues. I had relationship problems, and I felt like life was a battle. At that time, I believed that every day I needed to get up and fight. I had to fight for peace and fight for a sound mind. I was emotionally unstable and physically drained. I was gaining weight uncontrollably, and I was miserable. I didn't like who I had become; my life did not reflect what I desired it to be. I wanted to be happy, adventurous, healthy, financially stable, and fun. I was tired of being sad and disappointed. I was consistently faced with closed doors to much of what I desired. I was getting everything I didn't want and missing out on everything I did want. It got to the point where I became desperate for help. I sought out any and everyone who could help—doctors, psychiatrist, therapists, pastors, ministers, friends, and family—and I learned a very valuable lesson. I learned that no one in this external world has all the answers to your internal pain, and to heal internal trauma you must seek the divine guidance inside of yourself. While you can gain inspiration and some direction from others, your complete healing starts by listening within.

Once I stopped seeking external answers and started listening to that small inner voice through prayer, meditation, and following my intuition, I realized my mind, body, and soul needed nourishment. I took that disparate energy I used to seek guidance externally and redirected that energy toward investing in myself mentally, physically, and emotionally. Every morning I did something to nurture my mind, body, and spirit. To gain control of my thoughts and enhance my mental health I would speak positive affirmations, listen to positive messages, and meditate. I would nurture my spirit and emotion by writing a gratitude list and praying prayers of love and appreciation. I also made a daily commitment to my physical fitness by exercising and eating healthy foods. This mind, body, and soul routine became my daily habits of happiness. In the beginning it felt weird and awkward, but I felt better and better each day. I started to look forward to "me time," and it led me to become a new person; little by little I started to like myself more. I discovered that much of the pain and the childhood trauma I struggled with was a result of the battle I had with myself. After consistently nurturing my mind, body, and soul day after day, and as the days turned into months, I began to value myself more and more. My daily intentional habits of happiness led to me hiring a personal trainer and an emotional coach. These individuals played a major role in supporting my goals and providing accountability. I learned more about nutrition and how energy and my vibrational attitude impacts my life. I released over 35 pounds and became physically fit; I improved my relationships and gained a stronger connection with my husband and kids; and my finances and career opportunities enhanced and multiplied.

***

I learned that your thoughts create your beliefs, your beliefs create your words, your words create your actions, and your actions create your reputation and character. Finally, your reputation and character give life to your destiny. Your destiny is your future; it's where you are headed. What you do today will determine your tomorrow. It's important to understand the key principals to happiness and being the best version of yourself.

***

The key principals to happiness that allow me to live a life of health and happiness are the following:

1. Be intentional.
2. Have a vision for your life.
3. Be confident.
4. Get support.
5. Be aware of your attitude.

BE INTENTIONAL

A major turning point in my life and the expansion of my level of happiness occurred when I became more intentional about what I really wanted in life. Before that I would just go with the flow and deal with whatever came in my life. This led me to reacting to whatever issues and problems come up instead of being proactive about making decisions and taking action toward what I desired to create in my life. I had to become more purposeful about building my life around my core values, desires, and beliefs. I needed to stop acting on impulse and start living with intention. I also had to stop doing things just because of tradition and childhood rituals that were enforced by my parents that no longer served me. For example, as much as I love my spiritual connection through prayer and meditation, I discovered that I had a much deeper bond with God in my quiet moments of prayer alone and during a family devotion at home than I did attending an organized religious ceremony with hundreds of people on Sundays. Being more intentional led me to question why I did the things I did in my life and what the results of those things were. This allowed me to be more committed and focused on the things that were important to me. Being intentional empowers you to envision what you desire to experience in your future, and it gives you the benefit of being proactive about the results you want to achieve from your actions. Intentionality gives you a head start on creating the life you desire. However, a life without intention can lead you to take on too much and become easily distracted.

When you have an intentional commitment to what you want, your actions will align with your goals.

When I got clearer on the results I desired in my life, that new goal-oriented mindset led me to experience more of my desires.

HAVE A VISION FOR YOUR LIFE

To create a vision for your life, you must first start by asking yourself, "What is important to me, what do I desire to experience, and what would my life look like when it's achieved?" Developing your vision for your life will require you to tap into your intuition. That small quiet inner voice is often leading and guiding, but if you don't make time to listen and get still, you will feel lost and uncertain about what's best for your life. It's important to get clear on what is important to you. What type of life do you desire in your future, and how do you want your future self to feel and do? You only have one life; it's yours, and no one else can live it for you. Your life doesn't belong to anyone else, and you are responsible for the life you live. Although you are not at fault with what other people do to you, as an adult you are responsible for what you continue to allow and how you choose to respond to what people do to you. All of these things impact the unfolding of the vision for your life, and that's why it's vital to take ownership of it. The vision for your life is a guided inspired description of your future goals and what you desire to accomplish. As you get more clear on what inspires you and become more specific about what that looks like in your life, that clarity will lead to an overview vision for your life. If you could create the life you truly desire to live, what does that look like in ten years, and how can you begin to take the necessary steps to move in that direction?

BE CONFIDENT

As you progress, improve, and evolve in your life, you will soar to new levels that may seem beyond what you ever imagined, and when you are elevated it's important that you are confident. Having a healthy level of confidence will influence more happiness in your life. According to a study from the National Institutes of Health (NIH), "the term imposter syndrome has been defined as a behavioral health phenomenon described as self-doubt of intellect, skills or accomplishments among high-achieving individuals." Imposter syndrome was first observed as common feelings among successful women and other marginalized groups, according to psychologists Suzanne Imes, PhD, and Pauling Rose Clance, PhD.

A lack of confidence will hold you back. As you set the vision for your life and where you want to go, it's important that you are confident that you can get there. Real confidence requires your effort and your self-recognition. You must embrace your uniqueness, know who you are, and instead of seeking validation from others, validate yourself. Celebrate what makes you different and embrace that fully. Stop waiting on people to recognize and see you and your worth and start honoring and celebrating who you are. Your confidence will grow when you stop comparing yourself.

Comparison is the thief of joy.

—Theodore Roosevelt

Pay attention whenever you feel that people are above you or below you in some particular way. Your goal should never be to compete with another person but instead, focus on the goal to improve yourself each day. As you focus on being the best version of yourself by improving the person you were yesterday, your confidence will expand as you are more aware of your improvement.

Setting healthy boundaries in your relationships will also boost your confidence. When you feel like you have no control over how people treat you, it can cause a lack of confidence. Creating healthy boundaries in your relationships will help you determine which behaviors you will tolerate and which ones you won't. Establishing boundaries will also improve your psychological safety and provide more feelings of being in control. It's important to say no to the things you don't want to do, speak up when someone oversteps their boundaries, and make your expectations clear. Finally, it's important to choose to be confident. Sometimes you have to just act as if you are confident even if you don't feel confident. Ask yourself, How would I speak in this meeting if I was confident? What decision would I make if I was confident?

Would your posture change? How would you walk into a meeting, lead that presentation, or share your ideas if you did it confidently? A small shift in your demeanor can make a huge difference.

GET SUPPORT

Who do you need to support you on your journey to a more fulfilled life? Will you need the support of a therapist, personal trainer, mentor, friend, or teacher? We all need emotional support from time to time, and giving and receiving it can be beneficial. It's widely known that the best way to improve your skills is to surround yourself with people who are more experienced and talented in that skill (fitness, yoga, tennis, leadership, etc.). In the beginning you will work hard and struggle to learn the fundamentals, but eventually you will get better. As you commit your life to daily habits of happiness, it's important that you surround yourself with positive people who will support you in maintaining those habits. Life can get hard sometimes, and it helps to have positive people who can cheer you on during those tough moments. Spend quality time with friends and family who support you. When you become intentional about surrounding yourself with those who can share in your wins and give you positive feedback and support, it can boost your confidence and motivation to continue in your progression. Negative people have a negative impact on your attitude. Therefore, it's best to limit the conversations and time spent with negative people by creating boundaries.

You are the average of the five people you spend the most time with.

—Jim Rohn

Spending time with positive, happy, and healthy people will support you in becoming more happy, positive, and healthy. Relationships impact your level of happiness. According to writer Dr. David R. Hamilton, studies have shown that positive people live seven or more years longer than negative people. Positive people have fewer chronic health issues and are better at fighting off diseases. Do your best to limit time with negative people by making a conscious effort to set boundaries.

BE AWARE OF YOUR ATTITUDE

It's your attitude toward life and people that will determine your level of happiness. What you expect, what you feel, and who you will be are manifested through your attitude. The attitude you have about life is a force, and it is the power you use to create events in your life. It's important to show up as the best version of yourself. See people and events as they are, not as your clouded emotional illusion assume they are. When you decide to show up consistently as the best version of who you are, it gives you an opportunity to inspire people where they are. You never know when someone needs you to be your best. When it comes to your attitude, it's important to understand that it's ok to feel bad sometimes because emotions come and go. Having disagreements is also normal, and not every conflict in a relationship means failure. It's ok to not agree and to talk through those disagreements. There will be some days when you will not feel happy, and that's ok. However, I do want to let you know that you can choose happiness even when you don't feel it. Choose happiness by doing things you enjoy. Happiness is a choice, and it's something you do. Having a happy life is not about feeling happy all the time. A happy life is making the deliberate decision to have more positivity than pain. It's a life of more meaning and purpose, filled with various experiences that enhance you mentally, spiritually, and emotionally.

***

Your daily habits are creating your destiny. The truth about destiny is that nothing is prewritten for you. The consistent movement you make in your life leads to what's meant for you. Your destiny is a constant evolution. You don't need to sit and wait for it. It's your constant evolvement and discovery as you move forward in your life each day. The decisions you make and the actions you take create your destiny. It is not predetermined and out of your control. You can be deliberate and persistent in working out daily and eating healthy balanced meals, and those committed habits will create a destiny of physical fitness. As you plan a routine around your habits of happiness, make the decision to trust your intuition. Tapping into your intuition will guide you in decision making. Your intuition is like a muscle; you have to work it and exercise it in order to strengthen its clarity.

As you apply the daily habits of happiness by investing in your mind, body, and soul, this will allow you to become a magnet for positive relationships, develop a goal-driven focus, and build a momentum of joy. Taking this time to journal and ask yourself the following questions will build more certainty and create more direction in your life. *How can I be more intentional about my time, energy, and focus each day? How can I have clear structure in my day? How can my daily routine support my goals? What are the three most important activities that will help me achieve the outcome I want? How can I align my vision with measurable goals? If I picture myself having achieved my goals, what does that look like? How can I be more purposeful with my time? How can I set healthy boundaries in my relationships?*

9 | BECOME MORE INFLUENTIAL

There are times when we all struggle with the uncertainties of life, not knowing if relationships, jobs, and the state of the economy will work in our favor. Things can be challenging when working and striving to achieve your definition of success. This desire to have more control of your life can cause you to want to be more influential. Gaining more influence allows you to have more support from people in the journey of understanding what you care about, and it motivates them to take action in the direction of your vision. However, before you can be an influential person, people must believe in you, want to follow you, be interested in listening to you, and be inspired to act after hearing you speak. To gain the support and respect of others, you must first have a deep belief, regard, and respect for yourself. You must become committed to fully developing yourself as a leader. If you struggle with self-control, insecurities, and low self-esteem or you live an unstable, chaotic life causing you to procrastinate, you may struggle with gaining influence.

The best way to gain influence is to first influence yourself.

According to research from the Science of People, confidence is what helps people to be more influential, and having a successful daily routine is part of building confidence. As you implement the daily self-care habits reinforced in this book, by nurturing your mind, body, and spirit, this will boost your confidence.

According to *Business Insider*, Twitter founder Jack Dorsey has a morning routine of meditation, exercise, coffee, rest, and reflection.

> I look to build a lot of consistent routines. Same thing every day.
>
> —Jack Dorsey

Influential people understand how to prepare their minds for life's battles; they know who they are and are comfortable thriving in their strengths and acknowledging their weaknesses; and they speak their truth unapologetically.

PREPARE YOUR MIND FOR BATTLE

No matter what you're going through in your life, you can elevate yourself above the battlefield. In order to do this, you must first declutter and detoxify your mind of negativity. You can clear the negative thoughts through meditation, speaking positive affirmations, and journaling and therapy if needed. This clearing process can vary for different people, but it's best to do what works best for you. This is a process of healing and releasing resentment and other negative emotions that weigh you down. It's also best to work toward forgiving people who have disappointed you. Forgiveness is more about freeing yourself for the burden of resentment and making room for love. When you chose to forgive, you chose to heal. Once you are clear of the emotional baggage, start analyzing your current situation and focus on your long-term goals while not being distracted by the surface-level immediate situation. If you're struggling in a negative relationship and it's draining and consuming much of your time and attention, it's important to first calm your mind through clearing techniques like meditation, journaling, or therapy. Once the urgency of the situation has faded, get clear on your long-term goals and acknowledge the important boundaries needed that will support your goals. Keeping your goals at the front of your mind makes it much easier to decide when to act and when to walk away. Our success and failures in life can be traced back to how well we've managed difficult conflict. It's important to see things as they are, and not as your emotions feel they are. We all deal with battles in life, but the greatest battle of all is the battle we encounter with ourselves.

✳✳✳

It's the battle with your weaknesses, your unforgiveness, your emotions, impatience, and pride, that cause the most pain and defeat in life. It's the battle within yourself that weakens you the most. This is why your daily routine of clearing negative emotions and practicing self-control and self-discipline will serve you best. It's important to be aware of your personal weakness and insecurities that can take hold of your mind.

> We become what we think about.
>
> —Earl Nightingale

Preparing your mind for battle requires you to take control of your thinking. If your thoughts are negative, you will become negative. One of the most powerful techniques I've implemented in my life is speaking positive affirmations. The more you believe the affirmation, the more of an impact it has on your life. However, a major key to successfully speaking affirmations is actively implementing tasks that support the affirmations. Otherwise, you'll find yourself caught in a web of wishful thinking that leads you nowhere. Your behavior should align with your words: "For the body without the spirit is dead, so faith without works is dead also" (James 2:26).

Spend some time in the morning and before bed at night to close your eyes and visualize how you would like your day-to-day life experiences to unfold. Visualize yourself operating in a calm, peaceful state and having the mental, emotional, and physical strength to successfully master your day. Then take the vision and positive energy with you everywhere you go and allow your habits, thoughts, and words to be aligned with your vision and energy.

KNOW YOURSELF

Getting to know yourself will require you to become more observant toward yourself. The more questions you ask yourself about yourself, the more you will grow to know yourself. Before you can influence others, you must have a clear understanding and awareness of who you are. Several years ago, during a time when I felt overworked, anxious, and exhausted, a friend of mine asked me what I really enjoyed doing and what made me happy. After getting silent for a while and really thinking of the answer to those questions, I couldn't find an explanation. That's when I realized I didn't have enough awareness of myself. From that point on, I became a student of myself. I started paying attention to things that made me smile. I discovered that I love being outside in nature at the park; hiking also made me happy, riding my bike made me feel fun, free, and adventurous; and spending time painting, reading, and writing inspired me and motivated me to be a better person. I also discovered how much I loved traveling and flying in an airplane.

✳✳✳

When your external actions align with your internal feelings and values, you experience less inner conflict. When you know yourself, you can make better decisions about everything. Understanding your intuition, your subtle desires and inspirations, and knowing how to be guided and directed internally will support you in gaining clarity in making decisions.

As you stay grounded in your core values and beliefs, this will also support you in setting boundaries, saying no when it's necessary and you mean it, and practicing self-control. Sometimes the conflict and stress that are experienced in life are due to not being true to yourself and who you desire to become. Often unfulfillment and unhappiness are a result of when deep down inside you know you are capable of more, when you have a strong inspiration to grow and evolve, yet you are held back by external situations and excuses. We make excuses to not pursue our desires because we have children, or because our partner says it's not a good idea, or because we are conflicted with what our friends and family may think about our change. For years we put off what we really want; we settle and become complacent and fearful of growth. When you are not true to your personal standards for yourself, such as having the standard to be physically fit but consistently neglecting time for exercise and healthy eating, it causes you to lose a bit of self-respect. That lack of self-respect results in a lack of confidence and doubt in your ability. However, being more of who you are truly, upholding your standards, and following through with action that supports those high standards helps you feel more alive and makes your experience of life more exciting, richer, and fulfilled.

SPEAK YOUR TRUTH

Before you can speak your truth, you must be secure within yourself, confident in your abilities, courageous toward your goals, and certain about your convictions and desires. You must believe in your truth and the importance of following the path of your life. This requires a level of connection with your intuitive thoughts and soft inner voice. It's becoming a fan of yourself and a life-long supporter of your mind, body, and spirit. You should always be on "team you." This is important because you can't rely on another person to know you the way you should know yourself. Understand your worth, know your passions, know your desires, and become an advocate for yourself.

You get what you negotiate. Whether it's your career, your salary, your responsibilities, your relationships, or your boundaries, you must advocate for yourself effectively. While speaking your truth and standing up for yourself may be challenging, doing so will help you realize your goals and create a higher self-esteem in your personal and professional life. It's often helpful for you to identify ways to advocate for yourself effectively. There is power in your words.

Life and death are in the power of your tongue . . .
—Proverbs 18:21

Your words create energy, and this is why it's important to speak your truth. When you speak your truth, you release the power of life through your words, giving birth to the force that creates the physical manifestation of your life. Your truth is the authenticity of the healthy, happy version of yourself. Think about what makes you happy, and how you would feel with great health and physical fitness.

It's your divine birthright to enjoy an abundant life. You can receive this abundance if you are aligned to allow it. Your positive, life-giving words are weapons you can use against inner fear and worry. All worry and fear are robbers of your time. They come to distract you from joy and peace. The feelings of injustice and resentment are also your enemies; they come against you by causing feelings of defeat and discouragement. The mindset enemies of doubt, fear, hurt, and anger are the enemies within yourself fighting against your happiness and peace of mind. This army of negative thoughts comes to battle and defeat you through thoughts and beliefs that tell you, "You are not good enough, and you're undeserving of happiness and success." When you become aware of these thoughts, it's important to speak your truth; affirm "You are worthy of good things, God's wealth is circulating in your life, and you are deserving of all good things." When you starve the negative thoughts of fear and feed the positive thoughts of faith, you create more joy in your life.

Not only is it important to speak your truth, but it's also important to stand up for yourself. Unleash the giant within you by facing your fears and advocating for yourself. Don't allow fear to silence you; set healthy boundaries, say no when you don't want to say yes, and never compromise on your high standards.

FOCUS ON YOUR STRENGTHS

It's important to understand and be aware of what makes you stand out. How are you unique in your personal and professional relationships? How can you leverage your strengths to be more influential? We go throughout life day to day observing others and seeking what makes them talented and easily viewing what they can improve on. However, when it comes to analyzing ourselves, we often struggle to recognize how we contribute to society in a unique way. It takes more effort and self-awareness to understand your own strengths and to focus on thriving in that area. We often get so distracted by others and find ourselves working to have the talents and abilities we admire in another person. However, when you pay attention to the strengths, skills, and abilities others acknowledge in you, this gives you an advantage to build on those gifts and thrive even more in your strengths. There's no need to spend much of your time struggling to fix or improve your weaknesses; that only takes away from thriving in your strengths and creates more insecurities in areas of weakness. Can you imagine Michael Jordan, in the middle of his career of being the most successful professional basketball player, stopping to take time to be a better football player because playing football was one of his weaknesses? That would have sabotaged his entire NBA career. When you waste time struggling to improve in areas where you are weak while neglecting your strengths, it's a form of self-sabotage. Embrace your gifts and focus on enhancing your strengths to perfect your abilities.

When gaining influence, it's important to strive for significance instead of success. Success is about personal achievement, but significance is about adding value to other people. Ask yourself, How can I add value to others? How can you be of service? In what way can you make an impact? These questions will assist you in discovering ways to make a difference in the lives of others.

Legacy is not what you leave for people, but it's what you leave in people.

—John Maxwell

Influential people are very intentional about prioritizing the important things in their lives. They keep first things first. Not only do they prioritize their mental, physical, and emotional health, but they make their family and close friends a top priority as well. It's very important to keep first things first and maintain a structured life of peace and stability.

The best way to gain influence is to first influence yourself. As you focus to be influential toward yourself, this will enhance your confidence. Your confidence is what helps you to be more influential, and having a successful daily routine is part of building confidence. As you implement the daily self-care habits by nurturing your mind, body, and spirit, this will boost your confidence. Take some time now to journal and ask yourself the following questions to build more confidence in your life. *Who do I need to forgive? What are the negative thoughts that are weighing me down? In what areas in my life do I lack confidence? What are my desires and what do I want to achieve? How can I start aligning my desires with my actions? What are the affirmations that are relevant to my situation? How can I speak my truth and become an advocate for yourself? What makes you happy, and how would you feel with great health and physical fitness? How are you unique in your personal and professional relationships? How can you leverage your strengths to be more influential? Ask yourself, How can I add value to others? How can I be of service? In what way can I make an impact?*

10 | UNLOCK THE INNER WISDOM OF YOUR INTUITION

It's the most powerful source that we all have. It's that quiet, small, persistent voice, all-knowing feeling, and ever-present whisper of infinite intelligence. It's your inner voice; it's your intuition. Your intuition is the guiding wisdom that shows you the way to go when you're uncertain about what decision to make. It's when those small moments of life need your attention. The moments in the car when it's silent after picking your child up from school when a voice says, "Something isn't right, ask him what happened today," or the subtle feeling that comes over you to call a friend you haven't spoken to in years who so happens to need you at that time. Those small nudges shouldn't be ignored; that's your intuition guiding you.

However, it's not common to follow your intuition. We have been programmed since childhood to ignore our intuition and put more trust and reliance on external guidance from the adults and authority figures in our lives. We are taught that we don't know what's best for us and that we need to be told what's best for us by others. You were told to listen to your parents, teachers, and other grownups who know what's best for you, and if you need answers and direction, research the answer, find the solution from books, and discover the philosophies of others. You are not taught how to find the guidance and clarity for your life within yourself.

> Prayer is telephoning to God and intuition is God telephoning to you.
>
> —Florence Schovel Shinn

But if intuition is the way to unlock divine wisdom and guidance, why do we ignore our intuition? It's because we are trained to not value what's been given to us freely. Your intuition doesn't cost money, and it doesn't require any work or effort; it's only required that you allow yourself to receive it. We are programed to not value things that come without much effort. When you have a subconscious belief that life is hard and success and happiness is obtained through struggles, trusting, and allowing yourself to freely receive the guidance to wisdom and clarity feels too good to be true. Therefore, we believe the lie that happiness, peace, wealth, and love only come through hard work, sacrifice, and struggle. This belief causes many of us to live lives of fear and anxiety while being unaware of our intuition.

UNLOCK YOUR INNER WISDOM

We live in a world of answers and information, with access to search anything you want to know on Google or watch any tutorial on YouTube. We have full access to find any music, philosophy, book, or theory that's ever been created, and we have the technology to get answers within seconds that took our ancestors years to find—yet with all these capabilities, we lack the guidance and clarity to the answers of our soul. We struggle to answer, "What's my purpose? And "Who am I authentically?" and "What makes me unique?" The answers to these questions can't be found online; these answers come through the connection with your intuition. When your intuition gives you an answer, it doesn't just come as a logical understanding or the way you receive information through intellect. The answer from your intuition comes with a feeling. It's confirmed with a feeling of calm, confidence, peace, and certainty. However, ignoring your intuition leads to various side effects that impacts your life.

Signs you're ignoring your intuition include the following:

1. Stress and tension in your body

2. Consistently doubting yourself

3. Living in denial

4. Life feels out of control and unstable

5. Seeking approval and validation from others

STRESS AND TENSION IN YOUR BODY

Ignoring your intuition will cause feelings of stress and tension in your body, and it may also trigger headaches. Your mind, body, and emotions are connected; therefore it's important to honor every aspect of yourself and make time to connect with yourself fully. When you make a habit of ignoring your intuition, it takes a toll on your entire well-being. It can also lead to feelings of anxiety and depression. Think about it—ignoring your intuition is ignoring yourself, ignoring your truth, and ignoring your inner GPS designed to get you to your destination. If you're at a friend's house in an area you're not familiar with, over an hour away from your house, and you got into your car needing directions on how to get home, you would turn on your GPS to give you the proper directions to get home from your current location. However, if you decided not to turn on the GPS and just figured out your path to get home on your own, you would find yourself driving around, wasting gas, and wearing out your tires and engine only to struggle to find your way home. This is how many people approach life while ignoring their intuition. They are overwhelmed, exhausted, tired, and anxiously wandering around life with no clarity or direction. Then they complain that they're overworked and underpaid, stressed, and disappointed that life is a struggle. But they fail to realize that life isn't a struggle; they are choosing to struggle. If only you stopped to connect to the subtle energetic guidance of your intuition, you would have the answers you seek, the guidance you desire, and the peace and clarity to confirm your inner wisdom.

CONSISTENTLY DOUBTING YOURSELF

Could the lack of trust in yourself and regrets from your failed past decisions be the cause of you consistently second guessing and doubting yourself? If you find that you have a habit of doubting yourself, it can also be in connection with ignoring your intuition.

A double minded man is unstable in all his ways.

—James 1:8

If you are always doubting yourself, you may be an unstable, double-minded person who is in constant conflict within yourself. It's the feelings of restlessness and confused thoughts, actions, and behavior that create conflict within yourself. You are indecisive and unsure of yourself. This lack of uncertainty and instability causes an unsteady, wavering character. It can lead a person to not trust themselves to make the right decision, which creates a habit of seeking guidance and direction from others. This inner conflict and uncertainty cause a lack of confidence and low self-esteem. This is why it's important to make time to go within, listen to your soul, and connect intuitively. Making time to connect to yourself mentally, emotionally, and physically will allow you to understand and know yourself more. When you pay attention to when you feel tension and become aware of the anxious feeling in your body, you can become more connected with what's intuitively best for you. This is how you grow to know yourself and trust yourself to make the best decisions for yourself. There are times when you may ignore your intuition because the choice you need to make may disappoint someone or because the answer does not align with your current identity as you know it. This avoidance can lead to procrastination or complete apathy. This can create a lack of growth and elevation in your life. This stagnant development creates a trapped, idle state that leads to boredom and a lack of enthusiasm for life. This is when life no longer feels exciting or mysterious but, in your world, you feel trapped in a reality that has you boxed in a hollow, unfulfilling, dissatisfying daze that you dread each day. The confusion and uncertain feelings are a cycle due to the lack of inner connection.

LIVING IN DENIAL

Are you in denial of your truth? To others you appear to have a happy and successful life, but behind closed doors you are resentful and disappointed in your life. However, you live your life as though everything is normal. You tell yourself things are great, and you appear to have everything under control. Your life is spectacular in the eyes of others, but the truth is, you are not living the life you truly desire, and no one knows it but you. You want more, but you're bored and complacent. You desire more excitement and adventure in your life, but you don't know where to start. The truth is you are afraid to get honest about your life. Embracing your truth is also important when it comes to your relationships. It's important to be radically honest with people and not be afraid of hurting others based on your truth. Our truth, power, and liberation lie in our ability to tell the truth. There's a wall of fear that's blocking your truth, and it's safe for you to stay in denial.

The denial has protected you for so long that tapping into the truth is like traveling into the unknown. What could truth really give you? What if you didn't just read this stuff but actually practiced it in your life? Would life really be any better? Would you become happier? What would your life look like if you were no longer in denial but truly faced your truth and took ownership of it? Could you really set yourself free and free yourself for more? Could more really lead to the life you dream of? It's a challenge to listen to your intuition because then you can no longer use denial to protect you. But denial has you hostage; denial is keeping you as a prisoner of boredom and unfulfillment. You are here to live, explore, create, discover, and grow. You have the desire to thrive and embrace the adventures of the unknown. There's so much more for you to experience beyond the denial. Embrace the courage of facing the truth and receive the intuitive path to your life of fulfillment and adventure.

LIFE FEELS OUT OF CONTROL AND UNSTABLE

If your life is constantly full of drama and chaos and feels completely out of control and unstable, this is a major sign that you are not connected with your intuition. While at times your intuition will lead you to face your fears and stand up to challenging situations in your life, which can sometimes feel overwhelming, following your intuition often leads to a more peaceful, structured life.

Let all things be done decently and in order.

—1 Corinthian 14:40

You can know that you are connected and aligned with your intuition when your life has more order. God is a God of order. Think about it; there's an order and process to nature, an order to growing a garden, and a structured process to having a baby. And you align with the power of God through order. When your life feels out of your control and unstable, it's time to eliminate some things, get still, get quiet, and allow the intuitive guidance of the almighty to lead and guide you into stability.

For God is not a God of confusion but of peace.

—1 Corinthians 14:33

What does your life look like with more peace? How can you eliminate chaos and invite more peace into your life? Whenever my life feels chaotic or cluttered, I go through a physical, emotional, and mental detox cleanse. I physically clean out my closets and cabinets, and I get rid of things I no longer use and organize my physical environment. Once my physical space is more structured and organized, I feel clearer and lighter mentally. I literally feel like an energetic weight has been released. Then I cleanse myself emotionally through journaling and meditation by writing down and releasing past issues and acknowledge forgiveness for people who have hurt me. This eliminates feelings of hurt and resentment and creates more space for peace, love, and structure. This is the process of a life of decency and order. This process allows me to connect more to my intuition and heal any unresolved issues that bring unnecessary drama and chaos in my life. Also, the intentional order and structure created in my life aligns me with more peace and stability in other areas of my life.

SEEKING APPROVAL AND VALIDATION FROM OTHERS

Our obsession with being liked gets in the way of our enjoyment of following our intuitive guidance. The excessive unmet need of being seen is one of the biggest causes of suffering. As children, we are programmed to depend on the adults in our lives. We develop a habit of getting attention and seeking approval from others. During childhood we also develop the habit to seek validation and acceptance from the people around us. However, connecting with your intuition and following the inner guidance and purpose on your life has less to do with other people and more to do with connecting to the inner validation of your soul. Other people's opinions can become a distraction, blocking you from discovering what's best for you.

Although it can sometimes be helpful to get feedback and insight from others, when it comes to making a life-altering decision, it's better to connect intuitively and get clear first before getting another person's option. Get grounded with yourself. This is your life; no other person can live it for you. As you learn and grow to love yourself, trust your intuition, and structure your life around peace, you won't need the validation and approval from others. When you connect to the inner wisdom of your soul, that satisfying peace and clarity is enough. It often leads you to the understanding that your silence is powerful. You don't have to always talk about your situation. When you stay silent, you avoid the doubts and opinions of others and strengthen your ability to focus. You can manifest more accuracy and become more deliberate in creating through silence. This wisdom gives insight on the power of a sacred life. Not everything should be shared and revealed to others. There's value in being set apart exclusively in your life and keeping some things only between you and God. Your intuition is the guidance that brings you to the universal energy of love. That's real power and creation that comes from within.

11 | RELYING ON YOUR CONNECTION

This year, my husband Patrick and I are celebrating twenty-one years of marriage and twenty-five years of friendship. I must confess, in the beginning I never thought we would be more than friends. When we met, we shared mutual friends and were in relationships with other people. We had a special connection; I would talk to him about other guys I liked and get his advice, and I also gave him relationship advice. There was a natural push and pull from the start, for sure. We talked on the phone for hours sharing our goals, plans, and desires, and we would stay up late conversing, joking, and laughing. We had an effortless natural friendship; our bond was very solid yet smooth and easy. There were, of course, times when we argued and disagreed, but we were able to resolve those issues within the context of our burgeoning friendship. There was never any all-or-nothing dilemma that often precedes romantic relationships. Our connection never felt forced; building any relationship takes time and space to grow. One of the most important indicators of a healthy relationship is trust, and the first evidence of any form of trust in a relationship resides in time spent together. Can you count on your friend to be consistent? Do they check in on you?

We never tried hard to force love. I could *feel* the difference in my relationship with Patrick. There was comfort between us. I now understand the basis of that comfort was safety. There were great times, but it was our intuition that informed our dynamic. We had the type of connection that was rare; if we went a few days without talking, I felt like my life was missing something. At that time, I wasn't fully aware of the impact he had on me. Our friendship was a gift during a time of transition in my life. I was a young girl full of dreams with a desire to explore the world, and he was the strong, calm, settled soul who gave a listening ear whenever I needed it.

After being friends for over a year, Patrick started to share that he was interested in pursuing a romantic relationship with me. He asked me to be his girlfriend several times during our friendship, but I just wanted to remain friends. He was very persistent in asking me to take our relationship to the next level, but I was focused on remaining friends. Still, he remained patient and respectful without crossing any boundaries, and I didn't cross any of the boundaries he set either. Then one day a powerful awareness came over me, some may say I had an *ah ha* moment. There was clarity and respect for the person in front of me. I realized I loved him. At the time we were only friends, but I knew the love I felt was real, and it was much deeper than friendship. We were going on dates, but we understood them to be quality time before we considered them anything else. As I now reflect on everything, there was an evolution of our friendship that progressed into romantic love. It was a gradual process of connection and love. We started with a foundation of friendship, and that foundation has been the support that has elevated us all these years.

Love doesn't require force and hard-won struggle. Think about the people you love the most in your life—your parents, your grandparents and children—was it ever a struggle to love them? No, I'm sure the love you have for them came easy and gracefully. Why do we complicate romantic love so much as if it's hard? Why don't we prioritize friendship? Doesn't nature have a process? Doesn't it take time for a plant to grow? Why are we too impatient to allow love to grow? Why do we expect love to be at first sight and when someone's picture on the dating app isn't immediately attention-grabbing, we assume they're not the one? What would happen if more people took their time to build friendship; could it evolve into a more loving relationship?

Real love is a process of connecting emotionally, mentally, spiritually, and then physically. However, we can become so distracted by the physical that we rarely make time to connect on a soul level. It's the connection with the soul of a person that creates the foundation needed to build trust, commitment, and deep intimacy in a relationship. People are starting relationships out of order, avoiding the natural process of the evolution of love, and are left confused about why they struggle with relationship issues. The surface level of the friendship must evolve into deeper and more valuable information for both people. Do your lifestyles align, and do you have similar life goals? Ask yourselves, are we able and willing to contribute to our collective well-being? Being honest about your wants and needs beyond the intimacy of the present will inform the purest forms of intimacy you'll ever know.

The soulful connection Patrick and I built at the beginning of our relationship allowed us to experience an irreplaceable bond. Our connection is truly an authentic friendship of integrity, honesty, and accountability, which makes it easier to rely on and trust one another.

THE CHALLENGE OF TRUSTING ANOTHER PERSON

I believe most trust issues in relationships have less to do with the challenge that is trusting your partner and more to do with the struggle that is trusting yourself to handle betrayal. It's the fear of being betrayed and not knowing how to protect yourself that hinders a willingness to trust. Your desire to protect yourself from the pain of heartbreak doesn't allow you the energy to trust.

Ask yourself, Am I mentally and emotionally prepared to handle disappointment and resentment? Do I have the skills to properly handle relationship conflict, instead of doing the necessary work to handle issues that may come up in relationships? People often resort to avoidance behavior like ghosting instead of addressing the miscommunication. No one is perfect, and every relationship has challenges to overcome. However, our society is too impatient to go through the process of self-control and delayed gratification, which is necessary for building a trustworthy relationship. Instead of struggling to trust another person, it's healthier to take your time in relationships through the process of getting to know a person gradually and allowing the necessary time to build trust. Trust is built through consistent behaviors that reinforce a trustworthy character. Trust is something that's earned over time. The challenge is that many people expect trust, emotional connection, and authentic transparency to come quickly. When they don't come soon enough, they end the relationship, never allowing the process of connection to strengthen.

In today's world, people are experiencing a diminishment of trust in the government, corporate companies, institutions, and communities. According to the Edelman Trust Barometer report of 2023 (https://www.edelman.com/trust/2023/trust-barometer), "53% of people see the country as divided now more than ever." The cultural lack of trust has led to increasing rates of loneliness, anxiety, and depression worldwide.

Building relationships with soul connection is the most important factor in establishing trust—regardless of whether it's with family and friends or the waiter at your favorite restaurant. The connection starts with eye contact and a smile. It's the small friendly gestures that matter when building trust. It's also important to be a person of your word and to follow through consistently when you promise to do something. Your consistency creates a reputation that builds trust. A disciplined life is an attractive and loving life. People who love themselves are better able to share that love with their partner and other people. When you are consistent with follow through, listen well to people, and show appreciation, trustworthy relationships are the result.

TOO GOOD TO BE TRUE

There's a sabotaging belief that may fill your mind when there are lots of changes in your life and things are going great. It's the belief that *it's too good to be true*. This is the thought that robbed my mind after enjoying an amazing relationship and friendship with Patrick for four years that led to us getting married. Marriage was something I desired and dreamed of for a long time, and now that we were married, as newlyweds, I struggled with the fear that something terrible might happen. Everything was going great, and I felt it was too good to be true. At the time, I didn't believe good things could happen without bad things also occurring. My mind struggled to accept all these great things that were happening to me. I found myself in fear of infidelity and divorce. This fear led to unnecessary arguments and conflict about things that were in my imagination.

The arguments would start like this, "If you ever cheated on me, I'd leave you."

"Why would you say you'd leave me; I wouldn't say that to you, plus I wouldn't cheat on you," was how he usually responded.

"Because I want you to know that I will leave, so don't ever try it and assume I would stay." It was imperative that he knew I was not saying it just to scare him, that I meant it and that infidelity would hurt me, spiritually and emotionally. Patrick knew that the basis of my insecurity, and his own within our marriage, was born from fears that existed before we said our vows. Ironically, we had to learn through experience that we were strong enough to get through that early period together. Everyone goes through the early growing pains; not everyone holds onto their partner's hand to get to the other side.

These arguments happened frequently in those beginning years and continued until I finally overcame my own insecurities and fear. It was the driving thought that *things are too good to be true and something bad had to happen* that caused the conflict in our relationship. It took years to realize that most of our arguments were rooted in our own insecurities. It wasn't that he was wrong, or I was wrong; we both were emotionally hurt and needed healing. Gratefully, our strong foundation of friendship, love, and support provided the patience and endurance needed all those years that eventfully led to healing. Many people give up on love much sooner, never understanding that things can get much better.

It is tough. There's no way around the work that comes with legally binding yourself to another person. If you haven't sought out counseling at every stage of your relationship, you should. Premarital counseling is a must. Don't be afraid to reach out for spiritual direction. At the same time, there should also be supplemental practices that you partake in together. Read books that help you understand relationship models, watch testimonials and biographies, and make time for discussion. A psychologist will certainly shed new light on parts of the relationship that can be strengthened. Patrick and I are advocates of all these methods.

Everyone's relationship is different, the same way that every person is unique. There is always room to grow and learn more about your partner. Don't ever think that you know everything about your partner; approach the relationship knowing that it is an adventurous journey with your friend.

As I reflect on the years of our relationship, I realize how much deeper and richer our love is after twenty-five years of friendship and twenty years of marriage. I know if we gave up several years ago, we wouldn't be experiencing some of the greatest years of our relationship now. It has gotten better and better. However, I now believe, it's not too good to be true, it's real and it's amazingly true. I know now that I am enough, and nothing is too good for me; I'm deserving of all the good life has to offer.

Self-sabotaging is very common in individuals who struggle with low self-esteem or who struggled during childhood in a dysfunctional family. The reason I felt that things were *too good to be true* in my marriage as a newlywed is because my dad left, and I watched my mom struggle from one toxic relationship to another. I didn't truly believe in a loving, stable, happy marriage. I had to change my beliefs and build the emotional safety to trust and believe that my marriage was different, and I no longer needed to struggle in dysfunctional relationships. I also needed to let go of the habit of creating and engaging in arguments and disagreements. Those behaviors and thoughts were sabotaging the life I truly desired. Getting to a place of receiving the amazing life you desire takes work. It's not enough to want something; you have to prepare yourself mentally, emotionally, and spiritually to receive it. I got committed to doing the self-care work of acceptance. When your childhood consists of dysfunctional relationships, it may be easier to accept negativity and challenging to believe in positivity. One of the biggest lessons I learned during my transformation was to embrace and receive the good things in life. My mind had been so conditioned to expect disappointment, abandonment, and heartbreak, I had to renew my mind to expect and receive love, loyalty, and joy.

We often think our enemies and obstacles are outside of ourselves and external forces are hindering us from the life we desire. In actuality, we block ourselves with our beliefs. If deep down, you don't believe you're worthy of the amazing career where you are doing what you love and making the money you desire, you'll ruin your opportunity by not showing up for the job interview or avoiding it altogether because you're uncomfortable with success—it's foreign to you because it's out of your comfort zone. And when it comes to relationships, you may struggle with two conflicting thoughts at the same time: you want to enjoy an amazing, happy, healthy marriage but at the same time you really don't believe that type of relationship exists because you've never seen or experienced it in your life.

You can begin to shift your discouraging beliefs by asking yourself, Does my behavior align with my goals? If not, what's hindering you from taking action toward the life you desire to live? Ask yourself, What makes me feel uneasy when I progress? If you accomplish more than you expected, does it feel like the success is more than you deserve? It's important to get clear on what's holding you back from the life you desire and that you take the necessary steps to help yourself grow.

As you reflect on your situation, maybe you realize that when it comes to your finances, most of your self-sabotaging behavior stems from the belief that you can't make lots of money doing what you love and what makes you happy. One of my clients, Beverly, who organized a mental health event where I served as the keynote speaker, shared that she believed she could never have enough money. This belief led to her getting into debt, filing for bankruptcy, and working a stressful temporary job. She didn't believe she could be happy doing the creative work she desired to do while also earning the money she desired to fund the lifestyle she envisioned for herself. Her parents subconsciously taught her that money comes from struggling to do hard work from a job that made you unhappy.

The uncertainty and fear of failure are what stopped her from doing the work she desired to do. Her logical mind accused her of not being responsible if she didn't work that stressful job. She also felt like she didn't deserve the success of doing what she loved. Beverly shared how after she started committing herself to the healing work of self-care, she began to free herself from self-sabotaging behavior. She realized how much she was forcing herself to do things she didn't want to do by working that job. She now believes she deserves success and good things in her career. She left that stressful job, and now she's allowing herself to do more creative work that makes her happy.

THE TURNING POINT

The one thing that allowed Patrick and I to finally put our complete trust in each other was acceptance. I had to first accept myself completely and accept the idea that I could enjoy the happy, fulfilled marriage I envisioned by first believing in it. I needed to do the healing self-care work of accepting my imperfections and brilliance, and eventually that led to me accepting my husband fully. As I grew in healing myself through affirmations, fitness, and prioritizing myself mentally and spiritually, my acceptance of myself led to my acceptance of my husband. However, I wasn't alone; he also did the healing work by going to therapy, speaking positive affirmations, meditating, and exercising. After committing ourselves to self-care, the complaining and criticism that we both did during arguments ceased. As we grew in personal development and self-love, our compassion, trust, and admiration for one another grew as well. This is the work that eliminated the fear of infidelity and divorce. I no longer fear those things. They are no longer a trigger in my mind because I'm so connected to acceptance, appreciation, and gratitude for my amazing man, and his actions reinforce more trust, love, and admiration. As I give trust, Patrick reciprocates trustworthy behavior and also gifts me with time and welcomingly informs me of his feelings and deepest thoughts. As I've built a routine that informs my self-care practices, Patrick has grown and incorporated practices that cater to his emotional, physical, and spiritual needs. We gladly share some of these practices, while keeping some of them for ourselves. Still, we maintain this open-door policy that provides us with a flowing sense of intimacy. Know this, what you give will be given back. When I was giving fear and doubt, I was receiving arguments that reinforced more fear and doubt. It wasn't until I gave love, acceptance, and faith that more of those emotions, feelings, and thoughts became my reality.

Another major moment of growth that improved our relationship was learning to not take things personally. Patrick and I both studied the work of Don Miguel Ruiz in his book *The Four Agreements*. In *The Four Agreements*, the author, Don Miguel Ruiz helps readers to understand that people's actions, especially when acting out, usually have more to do with how they're doing inside, emotionally and spiritually, than because of their problem with another person. Sometimes the other person has a legitimate reason for their gripe, but the difference in most situations depends on if both parties are able to recognize consideration even in the thick of a disagreement.

This lesson helped us tremendously when it came to issues we needed to overcome in conflict and disagreements. We stopped taking everything personally by no longer internalizing the other person's words or actions as an emotional attack on our identity. Instead, we began to see tough situations for what they often tend to be, which can be best described as an individual's inability to articulately express their feelings and the receiving party's inability to recognize or understand this inability. The disagreements and conflicts in relationships are not a reflection of your value. This allowed us to heal and have healthier conversations. As I practiced these skills with my husband, it helped me to set boundaries and have healthier relationships with other people in my family, friendships, and work relationships.

Creating boundaries is important because it helps to decrease stress and anxiety in your relationships. It's vital to understand that you cannot control other people's thoughts and behaviors. You are only responsible for yourself. When you set boundaries, you are establishing where your responsibility starts and where it stops, requiring the other person to take responsibility for themselves. Having healthy boundaries in your relationships is critical for the well-being of your mind, emotions, and body. Boundaries are often determined by the value we place on ourselves. For example, if your value is solely placed on what others think of you, that will lead to having unhealthy boundaries; if someone is upset with you, it'll cause you to develop low self-esteem and shame. You may lose value in yourself if you fail to please other people.

Another unhealthy boundary is believing you can't say no. However, to start healing yourself of people-pleasing tendencies that create stress, you can start validating yourself through the understanding that saying no to people who ask you to do things you don't desire to do is helping you to evolve and connect with relationships that are more accepting toward you and your desires. Doing the activities that you enjoy doing becomes more meaningful when you can equally value saying no to the things that don't serve you as you do saying yes to what you desire. It all works together; saying no to relationships that are stressful and draining leads to saying yes to relationships that give the peace and positive energy you desire.

CONNECTION WITH FRIENDS AND FAMILY

There's a difference between connection and intimacy. Connection is the united bond you have with another person on a surface level, and intimacy is the transparent, authentic relationship that includes vulnerability on a deep level. Having an intimate bond with another person is not common. It requires deep work of vulnerability and trust, and many people aren't ready for that level of relationship. If you have unresolved issues with family and friends, those issues will impact the connection you have with them. Before you can expect intimacy, you must first resolve your issues. However, you may have family who are not willing to do the work with you to heal or reconcile. In that case, you should still do your part to heal yourself through the forgiveness and self-care techniques shared in this book and make peace with yourself. If you decide to continue a relationship with your relative, you should implement healthy boundaries that protect you emotionally.

However, if you have created a safe space for healing and you and your relative or friend have a healthy connection when you are ready to enjoy emotional safety in the relationship, and you are comfortable enough to open up to them about your feelings, desires, fears and more on a deeper level, that's intimacy. Intimacy is when the two of you share the freedom of being authentic and allowing each other to know your authentic, transparent self on a deep level. Intimacy doesn't just involve a romantic relationship. You may have heard the term saying a party is an intimate gathering, which describes a small group of close friends getting together as opposed to a large crowd with lots of strangers. Your close relationships with family and friends are examples of the elements of intimacy. Intimacy is the foundational element necessary to begin forming and maintaining all relationships. You may see and envy people, in real life or on social media, who seem not to have problems or stumbles in their friendships and romantic partnerships, thinking they can do no wrong, but that's not the case. Even your professional relationships require a level of intimacy. Time you spend with a person equals time getting to know their quirks—no one wants to spend twenty years on the assembly line or in the boardroom with a person while never growing close to them. Celebrating a co-worker's triumphs and supporting them in hard times takes a delicate understanding of boundaries and discretion that may be even more tedious than it is at home. Know that intimacy is best when it is earned and sown over time and the quality of sincerity.

As a child, we are conditioned to depend on our parents and guardians. They feed us, care for us, and provide a life; they are everything. Growing up, not only did I rely on my parents and family, but I also relied on others like my peers for support, direction, and guidance. I thought I needed other people to guide and support me. However, after being hurt by various people, struggling with people-pleasing tendencies, and experiencing disappointment in relationships, I've learned to be more selective about who I rely on. I learned the importance of having an inner circle of trusted people I could count on. I also learned how to discern who's really for me and who's just around. I understand I can't expect all family and friends to be available for me when it's needed. Although I no longer depend on others as much as I used to, I still understand the importance of community. I understand the importance of social engagement and connection. However, when it comes to deeper intimate connections, I carefully select how to share and who I'm open to share with.

It's important to know you're connected to people in every environment. When it comes to work, there are select individuals that you are more comfortable communicating with over others. Understand who those people are, yet maintain your boundaries of what you will share and not share when communicating.

I've learned that everyone doesn't deserve your transparency. You can have a connection and enjoy social engagement while not sharing details about your life. There are people you will connect with who can only handle surface-level topics communicated to them, like small talk about the weather and weekend activities, and then there are others whom you trust sharing your work challenges with without naming names and sharing specific details, and then there are people who you know have your back and go out their way to support you; you may feel more comfortable opening up to them. When sharing your issues with others, ask yourself, Does it make any difference in my life to share this information with them? How can my sharing of this information with this person benefit me or this person?

If there's no benefit, I don't share. Sometimes you feel the need to vent and release the pressure of a situation, so you share for mental health reasons. It's important to consider therapy instead. It can be more beneficial to vent to a professional therapist who can guide you in finding solutions to the issues you're encountering. Having a community is very important; however, there's a proper way to gain support and contribute to the care of others as well. It's important to understand exactly how to best rely on community without sacrificing your well-being.

LONELINESS EPIDEMIC

We live in a society that has given up on community connection. Social media, video hosting technology, websites, and apps have taken the place of in-person gatherings. Now more than ever, people are struggling with loneliness.

According to a report in *USA Today*, the proliferation of loneliness across the country is killing our friends, family, and associates. People are breaking down in public and private. Experts noted that there tends to be an increased risk of heart disease, dementia, stroke, anxiety, depression, and premature death. The subjects of this research are people self-reporting to their healthcare providers. The U.S. Surgeon General Dr. Vivek Murthy has made assistance for people experiencing extreme mental health crises a matter of national importance and hopes new policies will help to alleviate the stress of isolation. Healthcare institutions and providers are doing their best to imagine new methods of care and intervention, but openly admit that they haven't encountered anything like what they're seeing now.

Loneliness is when a person's need for connection in life is greater than the connections they have at hand. Communities where true and trusted intimacy exist may not be readily accessible. Imagine being the person who moved across the country in the spring of 2020 but who had not yet had a chance to begin exploring their community before lockdown began. Imagine life for the essential worker who had recently gone through a divorce and their spouse was awarded full custody of their children. What systems are in place for them to carefully vent and develop community? There also exists the person working for a company that hasn't ever properly addressed the Covid-19 pandemic and hasn't had a chance to process the pandemic since that same spring—of course, that person has a heightened feeling of alienation and loneliness.

There's a crisis of disconnect that many are experiencing when they feel that they have no one to confide in or trust. Loneliness can harm a person's mental and physical health. Now more than ever, social connectedness is very important. Become intentional about reaching out to others daily, volunteer to serve others, make time to put away devices, and spend quality time engaging in conversation with others by actively listening.

Having a connection to a community can be very rewarding when it's done intentionally for the benefit of all.

It's important to be intentional about scheduling in-person meetings or joining fitness classes, support groups, and social events. It's also important to make time for friends by scheduling time in advance. Our lifestyle has become virtually centered around technology, and it's not healthy for us mentally, spiritually, or physically. Ask yourself, What impact do I desire to have on my community? How can I contribute my services through the use of my talents and resources? As you prioritize community connection in your self-care practice, you are adding value to yourself and others. It's *the love habit* that you have for yourself and others that makes our world a better place.

EPILOGUE

There are seasons of growth and seasons of planting. Please don't be mistaken; I don't think you'll put this book down thinking that you've solved all your problems. There will be tough times, but suffering won't last always. *The Love Habit*'s purpose was to provide you with tools to assess how you can better move through the world with discernment. Does this support the life I'm trying to create? *That* is the question you know to ask yourself, and now you know where to look for the answer. Your habits and the discipline needed to maintain them is what allows you the freedom to lead a healthier life.

My peace can be found in my self-care and my relationship with my husband, children, and extended family. That's top priority for me in this life. My bank account, followers, and degrees from Webster and Chicago State don't fulfill me in the way that the many loving relationships I've developed throughout my life fulfill me.

This journey of coaching women who struggle with negative relationships, guiding them to implement healthy boundaries, and helping readers achieve results has been very rewarding. I've learned so much. No matter how much I analyze social media, entertainment, and our news cycle's negative influence on our perceptions of what relationships should entail, I am encouraged. To be clear, I am encouraged by the desire to do better that exists in everyone I've worked with over the past ten years.

This past spring, I sat with my husband, Patrick, watching our son graduate from high school. Our daughter cheered him on and let us know she couldn't wait to graduate next.

Our son walked across the stage dressed in cap, gown, and his family's love. The joy was there for everyone to smell, hear, and taste. The clapping. My son's smile and laughter. The sun. I'm able to push myself to be better from day to day for moments like those. There is nothing that can compare to the time I'm able to spend with them. I understand and want you to understand that by working to better yourself allows you to be there for other people when it matters.

Be kind to yourself and keep going, Sis!

ACKNOWLEDGMENTS

Thank you to my agent, Michele Martin, for believing in me as a writer and motivating me to grow and embrace a new level of discipline and appreciation for my life's work. This journey has stretched me to become a better version of myself, and I appreciate your support. Thank you to my editor, Jarrod Harrison, for believing in *The Love Habit* and having a creative imagination that aligns with my vision for a happier life and healthier relationships starting with self-care. To have an idea and meet a team of people who are aligned with what I've imagined, who then also put in the time and effort to help me turn my ideas into a tangible reality, is such an amazing experience.

Thank you to my husband, Patrick, for supporting me since day one. You were the first person I talked to about my dream of becoming an author back in 2006. I was so afraid that I almost didn't believe it was possible; I had never met an author. I just knew that I desired to become one. At the time, there was no evidence that I would ever become an author, but my best friend and husband, Patrick Howard, told me he believed in me, and I could do it. That was gold for me, and today, after writing eight books, I'm so thankful for the love and support. Thank you to my wonderful children, Patrick "Bj" and Aniyah "Princess." You are the best children a parent could ever ask for. You both make your dad and I so proud. You continue to inspire me to be great and do better. I love you, and I appreciate you all.

Thank you to my mother, Lurena Frenchie, for teaching me to become a woman of faith and confidence. You taught me to keep God at the center of my life and to believe in myself and never give up. Thanks for being a loving mother with a huge generous spirit. You taught me so much, and I appreciate you. Thanks to all my family and friends who have loved and inspired me; I appreciate each and every one of you.

ENDNOTES

xvi *Data from Harvard University:* Center on the Developing Child. 2007. In brief: The science of early childhood development. https://developingchild.harvard.edu/resources/inbrief-science -of-ecd/

xvii *We are masters of out genetics*: Integrative Medicine (Encinitas). 2017. Credit: National Library of Medicine.

xviii *Epictetus*: Encyclopaedia Britannica. Epictetus. 2023, September 18. https://www.britannica.com/biography/Epictetus-Greek -philosopher. Accessed November 4, 2023.

32 *Communicate it effectively to others*: Karin Gepp & Margarita Tartakovky. 2015. What it means to teach people how to treat you. https:// psychcentral.com/blog/what-it-means-to-teach-people-how-to -treat-you

33 *Labeling can be disabling*: John M. Gottman. 1996, September. Parental meta-emotion philosophy and the emotional life of families: Theoretical models and preliminary data. *Journal of Family Psychology*. https://www.researchgate.net/publication/232602696

47 *You belong to you*: Brene Brown. 2010, August 27. *The gifts of imperfection*. Hazelden.

59 *His or her ideal self*: Suzaan Oltmann. 2014.

69 *Problems such as heart disease*: Kelly Bilodeau. 2021. Harvard Health Publishing.

87 *They prioritize themselves first*: Marc Emmer. *Forbes*, Small Business 2019, November 19.

88 *Simone Biles*: Simone Biles, Bloomberg Television, 2021, July 29.

90 *48 percent of nonentrepreneurs*: https://www.nimh.nih.gov/health/statistics/mental-illness#part_2555

104 *Psychology Today*. 2024. Love bombing. https://www.psychologytoday.com/us/basics/love-bombing

110 *Psychology Today*. 2024. Growth mindset. https://www.psychologytoday.com/us/basics/growth-mindset

123 Swarnakshi Sharma. 2021, August 17. Why surround yourself with positive people | How to do it. https://www.calmsage.com/reasons-to-surround-yourself-with-positive-people/

128 Rosey LaVine. 2024. Confident: 15 strategies for more confidence. *Science of People*. https://www.scienceofpeople.com/how-to-be-more-confident/

153 David M. Bersoff. 2023, January 15. Edelman trust barometer report of 2023. Diane E. Dreher. 2023, April 5. Why a lack of trust is so damaging. *Psychology Today*. Don Miguel Ruiz. 1997. *The Four Agreements: A Practical Guide to Personal Freedom*. Amber Allen Publishing. Adrianna Rodriguez. 2023, December 24. Americans are lonely and it's killing them. *USA Today*.

166 Nada Hassanein. 2023, May 5. A loneliness "epidemic" is affecting a staggering number of American adults. *USA Today*. https://www.usatoday.com/story/news/health/2023/12/24/loneliness-epidemic-u-s-surgeon-general-solution/71971896007/